Broken Silence

Errol Van Moore Sr.
with
Errol Van Moore Jr.

authorHOUSE®

AuthorHouse™
1663 Liberty Drive
Bloomington, IN 47403
www.authorhouse.com
Phone: 833-262-8899

Published by AuthorHouse 09/04/2020

ISBN: 978-1-4208-9289-5 (sc)

Print information available on the last page.

(To my daughters who are my very inspiration for love and for life.)

Acknowledgments

I would like to thank all of those who have believed in my aspirations and me. Thank you GOD all mighty; Mariya Denise Moore and Minyon Deanna Moore, my daughter; Denise Francis, my mother; Cenne' Carroll-Moore, my wife; Terrell Jamal Moore, my brother; Errol Moore Sr., my father (thanks for doing this book with me); All of my family and friends, I love you all. La Rue Records; Big ups and peace to Michael Redmon and Eric Metcalfe, my Tri\Kobra\Nonsense TV crew; And to all of those who have ever came to a show, purchased and supported my music, dance, poetry and entertainment throughout the years. Thank you all. We'll do it BIG one day. You better –Belevm.

--Errol V. Moore Jr.

Thank you mom for always being there, R.I.P.; Matthew Moore, my father (R.I.P); To Gene, Linda, Wendy, Matt, Phyllis and Rene', my brother and sisters, I love you all; Mariya and Minyon, my dear grandchildren "Poppa Errol" loves you girls; To my eldest son Errol who I have been blessed to do this book with, thank you "E"; To my youngest son Terrell, I apologize to all the sons of fathers who shared their dreams of becoming professional athletes and somehow we were not able to launch you in the proper places to further the opportunity you deserved. You fulfilled the discipline and physical commitment to accomplish your goal, but we failed to emotionally support you with good judgment and wise decision-making. Not because we couldn't see your potential, but because we allowed the issues of our own dilemma's to distract us at crucial points where you needed to be directed and encouraged. I love you "T"; to all who I have known in my past and in my future; GOD and my savior Jesus Christ I'll see you in heaven, thank you for the gift of life and mercy.

--Errol Moore Sr.

CONTENTS

CHP. 1   MAN TO WOMEN AND OPEN BOXES OF US

1. Definition Metaphysical

People everwhere...
Searching for a place to belong,
A sphere of acceptance...
Wanting, desiring love...
Belonging to something.
Settling for false fulfillment...
In inadequate substitutes...
Even as extreme as...
Sadomasochistic beliefs,
Trusting they are a part...
Protected within the group...
Or even an appetite...
That creates inevitable pain,
Emotionally and physically...
Yet accepting its lure to exist.

Trying to escape within...
To recognize the pain without,
Until...
The pain without,
Manifests itself...
In uncontrollable destruction...
Leaving disillusioned thoughts,
And desperate actions...
To escape paranoid behavior...

Resolve...

The mind and the body,
Cannot be separated...
The pain in one,
Will impact the other.

The two become one flesh...
A union of mind and body...
The death of a spiritual connection,
The pain of exhausted hope.
Didn't God say...
"He hates divorce?"

2. Found By Love

Step 1: Become the right person. Instead of constantly looking for love, God tells us to realize that love has already found us. God loves as no one else ever can...and if you attempt to build intimacy with anyone before you experience God's love and allow Him to complete you...the relationship may very well end in disaster.

Step 2: Instead of falling in love, walk in love. Genuine love isn't a passive, quivering mass of intense feelings; genuine love is a deliberate, intentional, honest, even painful giving up of self for another person's good. The love that walks is other-centered. Love is a commitment that "walks" with another person for a lifetime!

Step 3: Fix your hope on God and seek to please Him through this relationship. God's prescription creates an exciting prospect in which two people are actually learning to please a third -- God -- by the way they respond to Him and to each other.

Step 4: If failure occurs, repeat steps 1, 2, and 3. God's prescription recognizes the inevitable feature of human relationships -- failure. No matter what your situation, it is never too late to find the everlasting love God wants for you.

Remember...There are too many examples of promiscuous people, once having found someone in which they could risk commitment...only to discover the guilt and shame of memories of past sexual encounters are preventing freedom from enjoying intimate pleasures designed for marriage only. Most often this experience comes in the form of lost emotional involvement and sensitivity through passive or empty concerns critically designed to nurture healthy passions that build intimate bonding. These victims typically stray from commitment searching for missing elements lost from within self, yet projected onto the partner as the inability to please, stimulate or satisfy. Sex outside of marriage results in distorted perspectives, loss of objectivity, and disillusioned expectations. X-rated images destroy the beautiful bliss of sharing your deepest emotions of purity, faithfulness, and physical pleasure, as the subconscious mind steals from your chosen mate the spiritual innocence of a union blessed with God' stamp of approval, leaving frustrations, low self-worth, and unfilled passions. Yet...God is so faithful...he alone can restore hopes, dreams, and value to those who will return to Him and trust Him obediently...

There is no other way...He offers new beginnings...to reject Him brings only destruction, death, anger, and guilt, tools of Satan, used to keep you defeated, discouraged, and hopeless.

3. Harmony Discovery

Man and woman
Still caught in the dilemma...
Paradise missing,
Looking to each other
For solution,
Only to find
Disillusionment
In the reality of
Imperfect existence.
Still looking
In the distant...
To dreams
Things the world says bring pleasure
Only to find
The rust and corrosion of
Empty and endless attempts to
Replace emotions
Disappointed
No peace
No contentment
Ever searching
Accumulation of material growing
Knowledge ever increasing...
Reaching through the clouds
To the stars
Trying to grasp a look at
Heaven

Man on Mars, on the Moon
No trace of life
More question of what is beyond
God, is not in the stars
He is unreachable...
Our efforts so vain, so futile
Look to his word...
For he is not in things we can touch
We are looking outer,
But He...is deeper,
In the mystery of the heart

In things within, that cannot be seen...
Only experienced in truth and love...
In the spirit.

You wonder why a smile
Illuminates your day...
How new love...
Creates a journey of
Anticipation for a lifetime
Excitedly waiting for...
Another moment to experience
Laughter, touching,
Looking into the eyes of a stranger...
That has become a friend...
The world suddenly reduced to...
Precious conversation of
Intimate desires and passions,
Long unfulfilled...
Possibility of sharing
A thought, a secret,
Safely revealed in confident trust...
Suddenly,
Hurts of past
No longer seem important...
Discovering the secret place of...
The highest God.

Alone, we are a note...
Together, we are a song...
With God,
We are a symphony...
He never takes away...
As some would suppose...
He is always increasing,
For those who truly know,
And safely listen to
His voice...
He is not in...
The thunder,
Not in the earthquake,
They simply obey

E.V.M.

His will...
He is
In the quiet, still, small voice
Revealed truth...
In you...
In me.

4. Find Me

Man and Woman, still caught in the dilemma of paradise missing...
Looking to each other for solution, only to find disillusionment in the
Reality of... imperfect existence. Still looking in the distant... to dreams, things the
World says bring pleasure... only to find the rust and corrosion of empty
And endless attempts to replace emotions disappointed. No Peace, no contentment
Ever searching, accumulation of material growing, knowledge ever increasing... reaching to the Clouds, trying to grasp a look at Heaven.

Man on Mars, on the Moon, no trace of life, more question of what is
Beyond. God is not in the stars, he is unsearchable... our efforts so vain,
So futile. Look to his Word...for he is not in things we can touch.
We are looking outer, but he... is deeper, in the mystery of the heart, in things
Within that cannot be seen ... only experienced in truth and love...in the spirit.

You wonder why a smile illuminates your day...how new love... creates a journey of
Anticipation...excitedly waiting for... another moment to experience laughter, touching, looking
Into the eyes of some stranger...that has become a friend...the world suddenly reduced
To precious conversation of intimate desires and passions long unfulfilled... possibility of
Sharing a thought...a secret...safely revealed in confident trust...suddenly hurts of past no
Longer seem important...discovering the secret place of the most high God.

Alone we are a note...together we are a song...with God...we are a symphony...he never takes
Away as some would suppose...he is always increasing for those who truly know and safely listen
To his voice. He is not in the thunder, not in the earthquake, they simply obey his will...he is in the
Quiet, still, small voice revealed... truth in you...in me.

By Errol V. Moore Sr.

5. Dynamic Tension

Misplaced anger can be the result of invested emotion outside the boundaries of a commitment or vow by an individual that has compromised his or her trust to a relationship, contributed to skewed objectivity in assessment of truth and fact, for the desired pleasure which is typically unrealistic or fantasy. When we have delusions of grandeur, " the grass is greener on the other side" or beliefs we are above or self exalted beyond the reality of committed intimate relationship, typically defined as " outgrowing ones mate", we have allowed societies standards to supersede moral obligations, and mores become convenient thinking to satisfy idealistic pursuits of popular acceptance within the tolerance of compromised values. The norm of coexistence in proper evaluation is bitter and sweet, where the bad is accepted along with the good, and when we escape to avoid this reality, emotion is leading decisiveness in selfish reasoning, instead of rational processing. Daily issues of relational development allows for growth and expansion of influences within the sphere scope of society interaction, and through difficult trials that test the direction of progress of individual adjustment for participants in mutual tasks, the ability to be submissive becomes overwhelming for the immature person and selfishness becomes their design for control of, my threatened identity, within the freedom of individual choice. The lacking ingredient is always the outside source discovery, the person or persons not invested in the construction of the family unit, but one who has crossed forbidden territory with selfish motives that offer a false solution of relief from the disciplines of sacrificial obligations that appear to be an unending task in the opposite direction of pleasures desired. Typically this person or influence presents itself as concerned with the frustrated wants of the searching or straying individual, or mate, and their motives revealing an almost relentless interest of attention and purpose, causing the prey to view them as a wonderful, good, comforting, and of course available, option, after all "I am my own person, and I have my right to choose." While its victim is being set up for the eventual let down and fall back to reality, to discover what has now become an additional dilemma to the original situational issues, and the false comforter, having greedily struck the death blow to the lusts of the unfaithful partner, unknowing to all interests is the fact that the dynamics have all snowballed down the mountain and are increasing in size and speed. We often refer to opening Pandora's box and the contents are now loosed to unpredicted dimensions of spreading problems. Deceitfulness breeds lying and contact with the truth is skewed and initially anger is turned on the mate or source of perceived anxiety connected with the daily issues that must be confronted. Often escape is the focus, defined in "I need my space", as the immature partner through addressing a desired gratification believes that someone outside the commitment has met their missing need, and the home wrecker for a season, appears to be a hero... but...as they say in the game of life, the fat lady hasn't sung, the game isn't over. Stolen waters are sweet, but in the end they turn bitter, and once the false comforter (lover...not), fatigues with the escalating issues that have begun to come in his direction and the investment of time and concern made available to conquer the prey is now causing complications with the freedoms of casual involvement as the strayed mate demands more interaction and the true cavalier attitude of the hero...not, exposes itself along with the realization of error in judgment only to discover the reality of false hopes and wasted time, while guilt and the awkwardness in facing the truth of the hurting, confused victims of the true family unit becomes a daily confrontation of reality undesired. Next stop on the ride to destruction of a dream is finding a way out of the commitment, so that the strayed mate can feel good about themselves again, after all, it's their fault I wasn't happy to begin with, and I never would have strayed if I were..."wrong answer", denial. Some individuals, often most, never return to a simple, calm, and peaceful life, and the patterns of shame and guilt leave scared emotions that only heal over with false solutions that give only temporary seasons or moments of escape to freedom from the deep hurt of failure and loss when a family is destroyed, and those moments spent in reflection and regret become a cancer to laughter and joy and precious moments that can only be appreciated through the experience of a successful mission that establishes a home full of love and treasured memories. Most of the time the false comforter has in the present life seemingly walked away clear of the destruction, while the straying partner attempts to find a new beginning, somewhere, but I can assure you without a life changing experience of repentance to God, this life can be an empty journey of loneliness while waiting for a reward of eternal darkness and separation from God. Marriage is a vow to God, and the bible says that it is better not to make a vow to God, then to make one and not keep it.

Most of the time the straying partner continues to blame his mate for his poor judgment, typically justifying himself with thoughts such as "if you had met my needs, I wouldn't have had to stray". And in this state of denial can actually return for a season to the marriage, and reason, I haven't done anything wrong, I wasn't happy anyway. Problem is sleeping dogs don't die, they're just waiting for another opportunity to justify unfaithfulness, and in the confusion of life's issues it won't be long before the selfish desire needs to be fed again. Often offenders will say, I love you, I'm just not in love with you right now...can you afford to wait while they figure out how they feel? I need a fresh start really means...I can no longer stand to look at what I've done to my family, and leaving the mess created for a fresh beginning doesn't eliminate the real problem...they have yet to understand, my mate isn't perfect, but the real problem is me.

6. The Fires of Passions Would Not Go Out

So often we begin our journey of years with the dreams of passions desired, and the ideals we discover in this mystery of life can fully feed appetites bent on accomplishing its mission of satisfaction. Addictions begin as seeds of thought, and harvest in out of control longings for their fixation to end that moment of craving want. In our youth our minds are methodically, and subtly filled with images beyond our reach of acquisition with boundaries our guides restrain in mentoring, and the fire begins to intensify with the curiosity of exploration, and approaching liberty, as a young man spreads his wings, and establishes a bent on finding a treasure of discovery that most often manifests in fantasy's snare of the search, and the dangers of pursuing exciting risks that are beyond the routine, and for many, the misunderstood boredom of discipline...more appropriately defined as delayed gratification.

Sex is the most powerful drug of destruction when it has been exploited and misused by the limited understanding of the consequences of practices outside of its design for marriage. The paradise sought after in its inception is as deceptive as the tide that is drawn from the shore as the wall of water builds to form a Tsunami...you know something is suddenly changed, but the speed and power of nature can so swiftly and destructively wash all perfect dreams away. Its victims can find themselves lost, and hopelessly dangling in suspension of dilemmas, without a remedy, when it has been abused, and imminent destruction awaits where shame and guilt have stolen all dignity. Over 33 million abortions numbered...when will enough be enough. The one hope that remains in this tragic development is God, yet those who continue to resist the obvious need for immediate change, still relying on self...self help books can't meet deep spiritual needs...will ultimately face death through health issues or emotional emptiness will drain vital substance of life. How often have you seen the anticipation of youthful energy invested in sexual encounters produce devastation, and disappointments, and the loss of an individuals purpose, dreams, and identity to cavalier individuals in encounters that drain the life blood of victims looking for intimacy, and relationship, only to discover the love given in hopes of reciprocity isn't even valued or appreciated, and the scars left as reminders are often fears a lifetime can not heal, if you are fortunate enough to have escaped the prison of placing life on hold for someone you're waiting..."to change."

In our youth we have often believed sex is a cure-all for loneliness and passions we have, and desire to express our being to another, not realizing the fire of these emotions can't be quenched with a glass of water. Truly...

all another person can be in this experience of life is a drink to refresh the thirst at that moment we connect, for the fulfillment we actually search for in fighting the fires of passions, is a fire that must be discovered in seeking the truth in wisdom in deeper depths of spiritual relationship with our creator as our mission, and purpose is prepared in His will for our experience. Delight yourself in the Lord, and He will give you the desires of your heart. How can we being finite creatures know what things in life will bring us pleasure? We are set up by exploration, and anxious desires that seem right in the beginning when they touch emotions that are hungry for relationship, connection, and intimate experiences we need for survival in this life...but we rush in to quickly, and fail in establishing value, purpose, and trust through commitment that is considered old fashioned and square...not understanding human desire is greedy, selfish, and without control the boundaries are never satisfied. When the balance of concern in a relationship for the other person's investment of time and feelings for you is lost...respect is gone...and all the tears in the ocean won't change a cold, hard heart and restore tender compassion. Someone will become a doormat when the flames go out...and balance becomes a sickness feeding only the needs of the individual with aggressive demands at their own convenience...as long as the passive, calm, hopeful, individual tolerates being controlled. "That is not relationship... you can do better... should think more of yourself...never to allow anyone to abuse your investment in them... and your affections for them."

Sex is spiritual as well as physical and in marriage you are protected when issues of life challenge vows, as they will in every relationship because we are imperfect and selfish by nature. The fact that the bonding accomplished through sexual intimacy outside of marriage is a pattern designed for mutual benefits that assist in multi-dimensions of a Godly creation, marriage, it has designs for success that are misinterpreted without honoring the laws of God that instruct a man and woman to marry quickly if your appetite for each other can not be controlled. Sex can keep a horrible relationship in compromise for years with the complications of breaking the spiritual bond that occurs within its pleasures of experience and its Godly purpose. The problem in most common involvements in the battle of man and woman falls to a conclusion something like this..."for men, sex is a tool for functional purpose for survival and feeding the ego of conquering the weaker species through an intellectual need for dominance and control... if she gives in to me, "I'm The Man." Romance is mostly insignificant to males outside of a device to entice the prey." Man is the giver physically in anatomy...but he is literally the receiver emotionally.. From her, needing her acceptance to validate (his world and being). If he knows she admires and respects him...he will love her exuberantly for affirming his value to her and the rapture is on...fact is, a man can't out do her love. For most women...for the playing field is evolving and many female "Players" think they can comprehend the game without devastating consequences...sex is an experience of emotions involved in the appreciation and gratification of a man that can make her feel her value and woman-ness...to be cherished, feel lovely, and desirable. No love and affection...no respect...no harmony. Woman is the receiver anatomically...but literally she is the giver as feelings and emotions for her man are expressed in her willingness to submit to create a blissful existence for the (relationship).

Sex at it's best is proven not enough, and we in those encounters will discover only...there must be more to it...even in the fulfillment of fantasy or erotic climax, the spent pleasure can only contemplate the next opportunity for the same moment of it's experience. Well...what is an addict? There is more to life, and you can't just stay in bed all day and night having sex...or sleep around with a variety of partners that are different to meet a euphoric need within you, the individual, because we are designed for intimacy in relationship, and self pleasures will keep you on a mission lost in a maze of opportunities, still looking for shared experiences of true intimacy that are spiritual, intellectual, and physical. Shallow excursions can't fulfill this need to bond, belong, even, to possess, only commitment that provides safety, trust, comfort, and freedom to be who you really are.

Have you ever wondered why week after week the nightlife is filled with drinking and searching for something more in life? Well, apparently it's not being discovered or if you could find what you're looking for...there would be no further reason to continue. It is an escape from reality and confrontation of self-actualization...who am I, and what is my purpose? Fun is often misconstrued as fulfillment, and unhappy people often laugh the loudest, because they need it the most to cover painful issues of emptiness. Alcohol is a depressant, not a stimulant as some would suppose in thinking a drink or two might relax me so that I can be or feel more sociable, and the truth is uncovered as under its influence we begin to speak the truth of matters that lay deep within our heart that normally we are too guarded with walls of protection to speak openly and honestly of, hiding often the wickedness of my evil desires. Don't act shocked...lust is the mission of social gatherings at clubs and night spots, and the pure at heart are not found reveling in secular indulgences looking for love to fill intimacy...you are being subtly compromised by deceitful pleasures that can be fun for their season, but consequences always follow decisions of good or bad choices. You ask the question...why wait? Did you know the bible teaches us, for all those who plan to marry or hope someday to find a special person of the opposite sex to share the wonderful experiences of life with, that in marriage a husbands body is no longer his own...but its his wife's, and the same for her...her body now belongs to her husband...it is a holy union ordained and created by God...can you see how far off the world ideology and trends of our society have come? . Everyday you hear someone say "its my life...I can do what I want...its my body." In all good conscience, "how are you going to live a wreck less life of liberal sexual expression with sick, greedy, selfish, people, then walk down an aisle in a church wearing a white wedding gown...to marry a wonderful person you didn't wait for...and live happily ever after."

Jesus offers you the only drink of water from which once you have drunken, you will thirst no more. He promises rivers overflowing with life, wonderful, everlasting and real. Seek ye first the kingdom of God and his righteousness, and all these things will be added in his timing for our lives as we prepare for his precious treasures he entrusts to us for this life. You will find that true love gladly gives itself to another...unconditionally, but it must be established from above by an infinite God that understands what we truly need, not by our own selfish motives and desires that lead to despair.

CHP. 2 *THE FOUNDATION*: PARENTS, CHILDREN AND LOVE.

7. What About The Children?

Have you ever wondered how Mary, a 12 year old, found favor in the eyes of God, becoming a vessel for the creator to enter the experience of a world and existence he created for man? Virtue is an uncontaminated choice to be separated from the common use or practice of society or natural physical experiences of this life. In those days it was common for women to marry young, reflecting the pure heart and mind of a chosen vessel worthy to be used by God. Wasn't Mary engaged prior to this Immaculate Conception? Point being, the time for excuses is long over. In it's statement of significance and purpose, man or woman specifically in the virgin birth, reveals humility to a deity, an omnipotent creator, prioritizing our purpose and submission to his plan for creation. We must set our agenda for life aside to allow his blessings for us to manifest in fullness instead of arrogantly insulting his love for us through selfish pride. For years, I have listened to young adults justify waddling in past bad choices and excuses for failed marriages and promiscuous lifestyles that have devastated families and ultimately our society. The truth is, we have compromised our hopes and dreams, just like Adam and Eve in the garden. Who hindered you on your good start in walking this journey of life? How can you turn your life around and start a new beginning?

Can you picture Jesus, a 12 year old, telling his earthly parents, "I must be about my father's business," then subjecting his eternal nature of deity to submit to their order of authority for 18 years, until the right moment in history, in time eternally? He did it for us first, and felt we were worth his subjection in humility to give us an example of how we should live unselfishly. Love is an amazing power of selfless involvement in obedient choices of eternal consequences. He knew his divine authority, yet submitted his power to perform a trade working diligently with his hands as a carpenter, his own gift to man for purpose, constructive, and productivity, the labor of accomplishment and results of reward. It becomes obvious that his knowledge, and wisdom, was not concerned with the passing days of man, but more to the perfect moment to restore hope to a dying world, past, present, and future, that had been separated from a loving God.

What about the children? Our generations are connected together with this same purpose Jesus came and died for, restoration, by God's design for productive and successful living under his omniscient will to glorify his purpose for eternal life and relationship with man. When a man finds a wife, the bible says he receives favor from God, he has truly found a good thing. It is not good that man should be alone was the first moment in creation God addressed his knowledge of separation from man because of sin. Marriage was established as a symbol of our relationship as the body of Christ to God's love for his crown jewel. A man and woman marry in holy matrimony and he blesses it, says this is good and smiles to reward their obedience with, "be fruitful and multiply." Within this order we observe the balance of two perspectives that prepare offspring for perpetuating the generations of man and the institution of the family. This is the highest order of design for success in this world system to benefit the individual, the couple, the family, the community, the nation, and the future unborn that must inherit this planet. Interaction is essential for development and productive goals, allowing man to live in harmony within the family and outside the core group, a familiar phrase called networking. One point, that is undeniable, men can't teach women how to be women or the counter-part, but our older women need to teach younger women to prepare for their future, not necessarily as housewife, for that seems to be a challenge only the most elite of women can comprehend, but certainly as nurturer's balancing careers and family dynamics with wisdom and love, not by looking for a man, because you will too easily find someone who will give only an image of commitment, while investment by the female can leave permanent responsibilities when a man chooses to move on, or she awakens to realize, he can not meet responsibilities of relationship and leadership, but rather building her life waiting for the right man to find you. You will discover that men want respect from others they wish to establish cooperation and unity with, this includes the woman he considers for permanent partnership, and when a woman doesn't respect herself, how can she respect a man. A women who respects her man, will receive his total love through recognizing her value to their success, and his realization of her worth will increase in time to precious hours of desiring togetherness with his blessing, his wife, not his homies. Remember dating is for acquiring information about suitable prospects for commitment in marriage, and when entered into ill advisedly or prematurely, one or both individuals are not prepared for the long haul required for success. Books are written about these unchangeable gender attributes, such as," Men Are From Mars and Women Are From Venus," but both are by God's design for completeness in marriage, and even when physical changes are performed, how can you change what is in the soul. You can even acquire similar attributes in behavioral patterns, but they are learned, but the innate existence will not be disturbed, for they are beyond our ability to change. DNA, the signature for life in every being and just as a tree will always be a tree, a dog bark like a dog, and stars shine at night, fish live in water, and birds fly, men can not give birth regardless of what a subjective mind convinces them they are. We, man is the only creature that can pretend to be something he is not and attempt to justify it by saying it's my right to choose. He has forgotten he was created by a perfect God, and he has never yet made a mistake, neither is your gender error or coincidental, but by His design, unique to fit you as he has done.

The team effort of a man and woman together confirm and validate, reinforcing principles and values through communication and consistency, whether verbally, a more mature form of consciously applying instruction through defining interactions of living or observation, which is the tool of the developing adolescent or infant. Quality time is ineffective without reinforcement of values and principles desirable to instill in offspring. There is no substitute for quantity time with children in instruction, love, and preparation for life they must experience, and possible only through spending time together building confidence, trust, relationship, and understanding of purpose of roles by both parents.

The bible teaches us "where your treasures are...there your heart will be also." We have lost our focus, in giving our children things, substitutes, that pacify them while we indulge in our own agenda's, investing in excessive comforts of life, designer clothes, cell phones, playstations, xbox's, cable TV and activities that create impossible scheduling and hours of commute time, lost forever...can we afford this? Rather than seeing our offspring as investments for their future and our peace of mind as we age, we send them out into a sick world, unprepared, emotionally, physically, mentally, and spiritually. When we inevitably face death, what will be the precious treasures present in those last days and moments before we leave this world as we know it...our family, friends, and children...or our possessions that we are certainly leaving behind?

8. A Mother's Smile

By Errol V. Moore Sr.

I watched the roses as winter slowly thawed and the branches began to stretch their length as buds began to appear...the ivy I cut back in frustration...it had spread out of control onto the neighbors roof, leaving me with a feeling of guilt that I had not pruned it sooner. It never even crossed my mind as spring began to say good morning...but for the first time in my life, Mom is no longer here to work out in the flower garden.

I wondered for months on end, how to fill the vacant moments I had shared with my friend since Dad passed almost a lifetime ago. Pondering what was in her heart as she continued on with a quiet presence, often a nod of the head and a smile. Life had left her unable to express even a simple phrase to communicate her feelings of being without her love of so many years...Now her season had come and the flower of life was withering quickly. Before my eyes, almost in a dream, she was gone...so many tears, so much emotion and pain, reflections of memories recalled, helplessness for things that could not be controlled.

Death brings a sense of loss and agony we still here, can't understand... but as we watched her labor, the gentle moment when breath had ceased, it seemed the smile had reappeared. Come Over Into Canaan Land... the voices of her children sing...three generations of love, a legacy left to continue the mission, as the Angels held her hand and escorted her into the presence of God.

The months have passed...life now has continued...the vacancy yet unfilled...

Today as I walked to my car, I noticed the leaves on the roses had increased...the fullness almost stunned me, seems yesterday they were still lean...As I went on my usual journey, someone I didn't even know smiled as I approached...suddenly it hit me...God was revealing his Glory, his splendor of the promises to his children...I saw my Mothers smile in the Spirit, in a stranger, as a message, a reminder that he is here...to help us through this moment to wipe away the tears. They say in life a man wants to find a mate like his mother...it amazes me to think how important smiles have become again...Now I see my quest, much like it was as a lad weaned from mothers comfort I had always known...Searching to replace the vacant place left in the memory of a Mother's love.

9.   A Light Can't Come On By Itself

In a dark room alone...the light can't come on by itself...
Pull the covers over your head, as the distant shadows move through the room and the noises outside make no recognizable sense.
I'm scared...but if I scream, the Boogie Man will know I'm here, so I just lay here...shaking and crying, waiting for morning light...sure glad there isn't a thunder storm and lightning tonight.

I can still remember lamps with wicks...
When the power goes out, they still give light...so do candles,
But everything today don't always work better...
Or is it...better work...technological advancements sometimes,
They're just easier for big people to get to.

Daddy used to know when I was scared...but he's been gone so long...
He made me feel so safe, cause...
I knew he could turn on the light when I was scared in bed, unable to move,
But he left our family for a better life...
I wonder if he feels better...if he's happy.
I heard his new girlfriend said he don't even have to work,
Cause she got a good job, and she knows how to take care of her man.
All he needs to do is focus on being good to her...
Wonder if that works better...
Guess it better work, he knows he should get a job...
He had to work when he was with momma...
She told him "I isn't taken care of no grown man", just before he left.
Daddy forgot I needed him to turn the light on for me.
Everything today doesn't always work better...or is it better work,
There're just easier for big people to get to.

Momma had to get a job when Daddy left...
And all those bills keep coming in the mail...and there isn't any food.
Her new friend takes her to work, and when I asked momma if he would be my new daddy...
She said no, "he's just a friend, with benefits."
He must have forgot to pick her up, cause she isn't home yet...
I heard him say she makes him feel so good...
He needs her to give him more time.
I wonder if that made her feel better...

She's been so sad since daddy left and.
She's been drinking to calm her nerves with all that extra stress...
Momma says if this relationship don't work she don't know what she will do...
Everything today doesn't always work better...
Or is it...better work...there just easier for big people to get to.
The preacher told us, before Daddy left...
To listen closely to his message...but daddy said he didn't believe...
That man named Jesus.
Daddy told the preacher our family loved each other so much...nothing...
Could ever separate us.
I guess Daddy couldn't see so well in the dark...
But why didn't he turn the light on for himself...
He forgot I needed him to turn it on for me...
So I won't be scared in the dark.

Old fashioned tradition or simple truth...
The Word of God is like a lamp that shines in darkness, even when the power goes out...
Everything today don't work better...
Or is it, better work.
They're just easier for big people to get to.

10. And God Put Them Out of The Garden.... Because of The Transgression

Having shared the information of Mary, the mother of Jesus, and the fact that she was the only virgin birth recorded in history, in fact the only one ever in time, being a young girl in age, only 12 or 13, according to historians and customs recorded in certain early civilizations, at the time the angel, Gabriel, brought her the news of the honor God had chosen her to experience, the young woman I was speaking to seemed almost appalled at the thought, and her response stating "I don't believe it", left me intrigued to understand even more. God is so pure and holy that his presence will not dwell in an unclean vessel. Sin to most people as a seed or thought, seems almost innocent, yet left to mature and develop into actions, becomes the very nature in us that separates God's spirit from our lives. We tend to think only of the physical purity, but virtue must also be in mind, thought, and in the soul or spirit of a person. Mary in her youthful innocence, not yet being contaminated by society of the day and its customs and practices, had met the prerequisite required by God. Even today we recognize the innocence of adolescence and the pressures and evil of society in 2004 that contaminates and leads to pollution of its victims. We must also note the importance of Jesus' arrival into Jerusalem, King of the Jews, and significant was the fact that he rode upon a young colt, no man had ever ridden and the message of symbolic representation to us...God's honor and glory, must always be given the best, just as in our sacrifice to him, we must bring our best to offer, before him.

Never the less, we must return to the beginning to visualize God's example for man (husband) and woman (wife), to remain in context in our understanding of relationship between the sexes in earthly terms of purpose. He put Adam to sleep, and took a rib from his side, and created woman. Adam awakening to behold her beauty, defines what the intimacy in marriage implies in its fullness, "bone of my bone, flesh of my flesh", a spiritual and physical reality left as a message to mankind to remember God's purpose for creating and uniting woman to man, because, it was not good for him to be alone. Can you visualize the naked young Adam and Eve enjoying life in the paradise of Eden, God's garden of delight, in relationship with God, and no shame present, reflecting on a toddlers free exposure and innocent beginning we are commonly exposed to with laughter and shameless joy. Did you understand that sex had not yet been explored while living in paradise? Yes, it's true. Adam did not know Eve sexually, until they were "driven out of the garden", obviously, they did not want to leave, but intimacy was established before sex was even discovered...they were innocent, naked, unashamed, and they had God and the fullness of Eden that made life perfect. A spiritual recognition of God's words uniting man and woman as one flesh, the first marriage. God defined the roles of relationship when he said that no suitable mate was found before Eve was created. He established her role as a help meet, meaning someone to answer to him, Adam, not God, that relational dynamic was already established from God to Adam. Amazingly to understand the original definition of a helpmeet, realize Adam's condition without his wife, alone, not lonely, and God's generous love giving him Eve, his helpmeet, literally, one who rescues. Woman was the solution God created to solve the fact that man was alone. In his infinite wisdom he established a communication channel, developing accountability and responsibility, the couple realizing their dependance3 and submission to each other. We have missed God's intentions. We had it all from the beginning. Woman's role as a helpmeet was designed to accomplish multiple tasks requiring immediate action for the purpose of harmony with in the relationship and ensuring the smooth flow of perpetual existence in the ever-changing climate and environment. This gift is hands on productive, efficient, and organizational to complete the urgent demands for daily living, and focus on self-empowerment, and improvement to co-ordinate family activities. Thirty hours must be squeezed into 24-hour days to maintain the level of energy living demands to stay on top of issues today. The family is stretched to and beyond its borders, and mothers burn out attempting to juggle schedules and careers. When a woman feels her role is less important, or appreciation is lacking for her functional contribution or the man fails to recognize her critical purpose in maintaining balance and sanity in accomplishing goals and successfully reaching dreams and milestones that marriage offers, we begin to look outside the marriage relationship for fulfillment. Man's role as a visionary can make him blind to his support systems and off balance, he becomes lost in a dilemma of attempts to establish or maintain authority dynamics, and too often over compensates by spending to much time away from the nurturing and development of the wife and family, often overwhelmed and insecure with the complicated issues of a world running to fast forward, therefore, shrinking in, to escape, and submitting to fear of being inadequate. The failure to value designed roles produces dissention and disillusionment within intimacy while the issues and responsibilities continue to increase and organization becomes impossible. Pleasures can often create a path of escape from these complicated confrontations within the family structure, and without intimacy, eventually losing its victims to independent or selfish pursuits that cause an inability and breakdown of communication, leaving un-addressed destructive patterns that drain and dissipate the family harmony. Women have fallen victim to this independent drive of self-accomplishment, in all fairness in many cases, for necessary survival and have placed careers over the functional maternal role in the family unit. She has taken on more obligations than is required or expected in a means to become a provider or visionary, frequently because of the lack of men to perform his proper role. Society is out of balance because family structure is off balance, and moral decay is creating an irreversible decline in our world value. What will our children and the unborn generations inherit as a model or legacy of existence after we are gone? Responsibility is when you think about it before you do it, because accountability afterwards is often to late. Man blamed God for the woman he gave me, and she blamed the serpent she allowed to beguile her... and God drove them out of the garden.

11. Let me tell you

My childhood was one of many changes and obstacles along with some very memorable moments. My mother was a young and tenacious person, who always had a tremendous amount of energy, which I believe she inherited from my late grandmother, (Eslin Francis). My father on the other hand was the exact opposite of my mother, a calm and mellow fellow of whom was very skilled in athletics. I learned a great deal from both of my parents as a child, the good and the bad. I also had a younger brother who, I realized early in life would be someone that I'd have to look after and mentor. As the first and oldest child, I was placed with the task of carrying an independence that was forced upon me and my younger brother, due to my mother and father's divorce in 1980 or '81. Forced to take sides at such a young age as to which parent to live with, was at the time a hard but somewhat seemingly recoverable situation. I would not have guessed the affect on a divorced child until much later in my life. I grew up trying to make my own headway as a young man picking and choosing while touching and feeling my way thru life without a father figure in the house. So as you can imagine I had lots of time on my hands to do just about what was at my disposal. When it came to my education, I hardly ever went to class during school; pre-school, elementary, junior high, high school it didn't matter where and what, I was a troublemaker looking for attention in all the wrong places trying to fit in, trying to find who in the world I was.

With this confused reality I managed to make it thru many levels of adversity such as; moving from home to home, exposure to men whom were not my father living at home with my mother, my brother, and me, school suspensions and expulsions, a failed dream to utilize my athletism due to a lack of guidance and direction, hopping from school district to school district, countless school counselor visits without resolution, peer pressures, gang, gun, and drug culture. Through all this though, I managed to pull out a GED, which I can say I have been proud but by no means satisfied with. I believe that, sometimes when you go through the tough and winding roads God, has a way of working things out in a sufferer's behalf. I have been blessed with the ability to grasp onto knowledge, retain and utilize its gifts, and have been able to develop a consciousness for song writing, poetry, and the art of entertainment. I have in my past and present day living been able to perform for thousands of people through the art of dance, rap, public speaking, and stage coordination\choreography. The combinations of these experiences has aided me in my true call, and that has been that of a mentor and vessel of God, whom has been an inspiration to many youth of today whom have been searching on the same road I once

E.V.M.

foot. This is the very reason way I am so driven today to never fail, to never give up, and to always believe that any mountain can be moved if you apply action to your dreams thru faith, love and respect for righteousness.

-E. Moore Jr.

12. Resistance Is Futile...You Will Be Assimilated

The title reflects the conquering forces of the ominous Borg of the fictional tales of Star Trek, and the fear this invincible enemy cast as the universe shivered in mere thought of confrontation with this overwhelmingly advanced technological species. I pose this question...is assimilation essential to the direction of productive growth and harmony of the populace or whole human race? If we were all computers it possibly would be the most effective advancement known to the technologies of the 21st century, however to disarm the unique qualities of individual culture would in comparison make every flower look, smell, and reproduce, the same color, completely losing the beauty of variety and creative identity. "How boring," and so not God like, understanding He makes everything beautiful in its own time. In affect this is what cloning has the potential of accomplishing if ever it "evolves" past its primal infancy, which to this point has proven failure and the hope created by fanatic religious sects and political platforms deceptive approach to gain momentum for false doctrine and essentially power and monetary endorsements has been abandoned or exposed as ludicrous.

However, to place things in perspective we might examine the developmental processes of the infant and preadolescent stages of learning in living creatures. Assimilation is the process by which development occurs and when constructive building stages are hindered as a result of inadequate primary predecessors involvement, another example is sought after as an instinctive drive for survival and most commonly a destructive building is established in the environmental sphere and negative patterns are then absorbed as developmental processes. The exception would be sheer drug exposed infants are born with disorders from chemical alterations of neurological functions, diminishing the capacity of normal developmental learning or the obvious, when a DD child is born. My thought is to focus on normal, functionally capable children who through the traditional family structure assimilate into the mainstream of society and by design of that core unit in the home are disadvantaged due to neglect by presumptuous mentoring. It amazes me to realize that by the age of puberty, most children have realized they are not ready to go out and face the world alone. They recognize they need a mentor (parent) to make the decisions of responsibility and to establish guidelines of information as well as discipline and order in a structured setting, but it seems many parents have yet to figure this fact out, still reeling, often from idealistic expectations that are crumbling with the reality of issues in a fallen world, and the emotional struggle of establishing boundaries and tough love for correction of defiant offspring. If a child senses doubt and weakness in parenting skills, you will have a problematic situation due to the dynamics of generational order becoming level or equal, instead of authoritative, and lack of involvement in communication and interaction creates a angry, troubled, frustrated child who feels lost, unprotected, and unloved. The acting-out concept can carry over into adulthood once established as behavioral patterns and allowed to go unchecked by critical consequences according to unacceptable actions. If you are exposing your children to a double standard, not introspecting your influence and methodology of training, in acting out they are actually screaming in actions, "help me... tell me what I'm supposed to do...somebody, mom, dad." Who is there to hear them cry? Too often today, other siblings or peers and collectively trouble is looming as misbehavior is supported in bonding activities that are dangerous and risky...that's what a dare is all about, not acknowledging the value of avoiding reckless decisions. When choices of direction and decisions are prematurely left to the discretion of a child, he will make the wrong choice more frequently than not...and a fire is burning out of control.

In an attempt to summarize this thought with an example of just one aspect of the vital need for a man and a woman to present a model of love and cooperation, as well as unity in the home, which establishes for the child a sense of confidence, value, belonging, responsibility, and accountability, consider this. The faithful monogamous demonstration of loyalty, respect, caring, patience, kindness, and love, between a husband and his wife is the foundation of loyalty established in the psychological development in their children as members of that family unit, that is creating attributes of human interactions that prepare or ruin them for their entrance into society. If trust is not a role in which children are allowed to participate in actively within the core unit, how then will it be established in the value system of utility and application in his life? Children are impressionable and remember, they will assimilate what you demonstrate more than what you communicate, and loyalty can be channeled or directed to the right values if lived out before them in love, or to peers or destructive influences that attract or draw them towards false comradery in premature liberty in making critical choices, impacting consequences affecting their future opportunities. One, two, three strikes your out...and a young life is systematically channeled towards crises that tarnish opportunity and perpetuates institutional correction.

In many families, " that are still in tact," the husband and wife are still butting heads and the children are confused because the roles are confusing. ": Somebody's got to submit!" A woman reveals her loyalty to God as she follows her husbands leadership, and " submits to her own husband," demonstrating respect and order of authority as a guideline for family development and harmony, not destroying his confidence by references to other males character you prefer...those men are not living with you and " the grass that looks greener on the other side," once you get there...need just as much water, fertilizer, and demand for nurturing and your time, as the pasture you left, and in essence...you're just starting all over again...and with the dynamics of offspring and resentment to the new man, your troubles have just begun. I have seen many women admire their pastor or some visible figure of ideal position in life, and even dare to wish their husband was like that man. Be careful not to offend your man with attitudes of dissatisfaction. What benefit can there possibly be for him to know you admire another man, who is just a man, and you will never know that mans issues by the way he carries himself in public or the way he dresses...that's why they call them images...you can't see the man clearly and a facade is easily portrayed without dynamics of issues that daily life require.

Women, "SPEAK LIFE INTO YOUR OWN HUSBAND'S CHARACTER," he is still growing and learning. Encourage, respect, and admire him and his authority, which is God given, will develop and flourish, and your children will also assimilate this pattern.

A man must first submit his leadership to God's authority that tells him to "LOVE YOUR WIFE... LIKE CHRIST LOVES THE CHURCH, and in that spirit of love he will learn to " submit to his wife...and children, by acknowledgement of their value as vital to your being, and especially her equal position at your side and the gifts that she possesses that far exceed the challenges of your tyrannical control as she is nurturing and developing the understanding of the family needs that must be considered and addressed every hour of the waking day. Did you know the definition of helpmeet in the original Greek form is "one who rescues?" Many women have indeed saved their husbands from themselves...when they have let them.

Children should be given every opportunity by their parents to be trained, educated, and spiritually prepared and empowered prior to leaving the nest, and it can only be accomplished through the joint effort of two loving parents in its most perfect design. To invest in the lives of your children as they are developing during the early years will save much anxiety and frustration of rebuilding a torn down self-esteem of an insecure young adult that life has injured, cheated, and polluted with its hard lessons of reality. We live in a fallen world, and even with the most ideal circumstances in operation, we can still expect adversity and trials in our family struggles...Satan wants to divide and destroy...but God turns up the heat in the fire under the refiners pot, to see what precious stones we will become with the melting away of impurities...so try to eliminate unnecessary disorder and confusion...they are not from God...and learn to laugh and enjoy the season you are allowed to share with your children as you teach them.

Live long...and prosper....

13. Pain, Emotions, Scars and Reminders

Hurt people, hurt people, and we can only teach that which we have understood, so again pain is a message that proves itself to be effective in getting desired results when a lack of knowledge produces anxiety and frustration when conditions of life are out of control or overwhelming. Fear is a direct result of painful consequences, whether physical or emotional, and the inability to overcome fears that are real or imagined can cripple the development of growing and learning processes necessary for living fruitful constructive lives. My father left home at 13 years old because his father physically beat his sons, coming out of slavery, sharecropping, and ignorance because of the acceptance of this harsh form of discipline to maintain agronomy. In teaching my older brother from what he understood, he would take him to a second job in the evening into night, watering golf course holes to help him accomplish his task and at the end of a pay period, hand him 1 dollar for all the effort my brother had contributed. Not as harsh as the treatment Dad had received, never the less, a hard pill to swallow for an adolescent with dreams of his own future. Me, well I was the youngest son, so my experience took quite a different dynamic, it progressed to mental control because it simply was easier to intimidate with discipline, thereby, confrontation had no opportunity and respect for authority figures was demanded regardless of error or unfair treatment. Train up a child in the way he should go, and when he is old, he will not depart from it. Fathers, provoke not your children to anger. I recall an incident in my life in the early 60's as my family planned to leave a small midwestern city in Illinois. Dad had bought a late model Ford station wagon and upon arriving at school to pick us kids up, in my excitement to get a classmates attention, I leaned out the window to call her name with a pride in the shining new acquisition, still remember her name to this day over 40 years ago, Penny, so that she could see the car my family had purchased. My dad, however in his controlling ways, raised his voice in anger or frustration at my drawing attention to the car and told me to shut up and sit down. I was crushed, couldn't he understand my joy, pleasure and pride in the new car, after all, we were moving to California, and this was big, really big for simple folk like us. Sounds like some of the fear of the old south still affecting the ability of a man and his family from celebrating a step up... man there were 7 kids, that was the first vehicle we had where everyone could have their own seat driving down the highways...step up, but don't start thinking you might be going somewhere, just simple country folk. I was 11 years old when we left for California, and leaving close relatives and classmates I had grown up with was very difficult as we headed for this new experience so far away from everyone we loved. I can remember arriving at my new school, Camellia Elementary, all my classmates were out of control and today as I write, many, maybe most are already dead. Adjusting was very difficult and something in the transition had changed in me, and I didn't know what it was, but I was timid and unsure in this new environment. I had never heard it before back home in Illinois. All my friends and relatives called me by my name, with the exception of my cousins in the south. They always called me quarter head because I had a round face, and I hated that nickname, but we only went to Birmingham during the summer, so I knew what I had to deal with during the weeks we spent there. In California though, something new had been brought to my attention, and I hated this even more, everyone was bigger than me, they all knew it and never let me forget until long after graduation from high school. I had a terrible temper and often wanted to fight and did fight boys that were bigger than me, and my big brother was always there to cover my back, but dad just never said anything, I guess he thought everything was o.k, but dad just never really talked to me. I guess he was so busy with the older kids and work, then there was church. I knew he loved me, but he just never talked to me unless he was giving orders or correction, but support, comfort and approval, was none existent in reinforced conversation or in a slap on the back of approval. You can't teach what you haven't been given to give. You wonder if history repeats itself, well, I'm certain that it does, almost frighteningly so...I recall my ex left in 1987 and for a year my sons lived with me in the home we had purchased with money I had saved from the GI bill for education, and at the end of that year, without financial support from her, I relinquished custody of my sons, reasoning I knew I would do my best to financially support my sons regardless of the failed marriage. In 1988, my youngest son was 11 years old, and as he revealed the pain he lived with under his mother's care and the man she chose to place in her life with influence and authority in their home, he described confusion, anger. And destructive patterns as he battled his fears frequently left alone in his room playing with transformers while the new love in his mothers life existed in a drunken stupor in the next room. After all, a mother's love for her children will always consider what is best for their nurture and development...yea right, we can be so naive, ignorant, or deny the facts when we have misjudged the character of someone we once loved. Viet Nam, and while my friends were all doing lines of heroin and who knows what else, I didn't even know what it was, but something I had been given made me completely disinterested in participating in the drug feast everyone else had caved into, but I thought I had fallen in love with a beautiful young French-Vietnamese girl that worked in the club down by the South China Sea and she and I even dreamed of being together in my country, even to the point of giving her money to buy an engagement ring, but the limited time I was allowed to interact with her was not enough to affirm my decision even though I did get counseling at the American Counsolet where they discouraged me from following through with our plans. After returning home about 6 months later I received a letter from my closest partner still in Danang, and he had mentioned that she was still waiting to hear from me, almost like I was the rich young Black American that could jump on a flight and return to rescue my love sick girl...I had simply moved on. When I met my ex, it was actually through a college friend I let use my car while I was at work and he picked me up at the end of the shift with two young women and the rest is history. Interestingly enough, that same friend ended up in prison for robbing a bank, guess he just couldn't wait while he worked to save money to buy a car, easy schemes and foolish plans backfire and I never saw the friend again. Does history repeat itself? My oldest son was first introduced to his wife Cane' by a close friend of his who interestingly is currently incarcerated for robbing a bank...did I mention my daughter-in-law is of Asian-Black descent...the spirits we open to never die, and can be transpired to another generation.

We have such a natural inclination to overcorrect as human beings and so often we focus on points of life we feel were inadequately nurtured during our developmental years, whether real or imagined by us considering we had loving, yet imperfect parents, but as the world moves forward it

Seems the sociological demand of future decades present difficulty in dynamics of structure in the family we can't quite seem to meet on every level. Interestingly enough, if a person doesn't receive validation in the family as they are developing, guess what happens to that young individual attempting to advance through life as a marriage partner or parent of his own children...you guessed it, they are in fact underdeveloped within themselves and yet are attempting to fill roles in life that require skills that are not yet realized necessary and chaos is certain if self awareness has not provoked a conscious process to educate the lack of knowledge in vital areas of growth. It's hard for me to consider being as effective a parent as my own were for me when I have already failed in the ability to maintain a single-family experience, and in the effort to build communication channels with my own children it seems life has presented another twist we are unable to predict, but an escalating fact we must learn to overcome and adjust to in moving forward. Divorce will destroy the adhesiveness of a people and the beautiful design God created to build positive, constructive, confident, and prosperous people from becoming endangered to every idea and desire of the lust of corrupt belief. In fact, the abnormal of traditional family or society has been embraced as the norm by present intellectual thinking. We raised my oldest son in an atmosphere of liberty and freedom of self expression and as I reflect his interaction and involvement with so many people in our sphere of social connection, I realize the novelty of firstborns is exciting and can be open to wonderful experiences of thoughts of a bright future and promises, but somehow the pleasure shifts as demands of life and more children arrive on the scene. Environmental exposure for toddlers is critical to their perception of life and early on the attitudes of a child is fashioned by the parents and emotional structure of their relationship in the intimacy of the home, meaning, if mom and dad are confused with issues of building their relationship, the children will be recipients of that order or confusion. If the atmosphere for the child is loving, the child will feel loved, if the parents are absent because of demanding jobs and lifestyles, the child will become estranged to his emotional well being because the human touch is what a child understands as comfort, safety, affection, approval, and the needed dependence on parents to guide them to maturity, empowering a life for a future independent existence in which another unit is constructed. You can work 80 hours a week and drive the newest car, living in the Pocket area, and dressing your kids in the latest fashions, but if you're not spending time with them at home, you can't touch them, and you sure can't receive love and satisfaction in knowing your family is safe and happy from a job or a fat pay check. We have left many of our children hanging in the wings of negativity, feeling unwanted, often desperate for affection, and in despair for a lack of validation or acceptance within the family unit because mom and dad failed to put selfish ambitions aside for the benefit of the children. Today you hear many people say its worst to stay in a relationship where there is no love between a man and a woman for the sake of the children. That's just another sad excuse for justifying giving up when the challenges of life are difficult, and what is actually being stated by a mate that wants out of a commitment is someone else has caught my eye and I want to know if what I see is real. Bottom line is this...your problem is spiritual, and the deception of evil spirits is blinding you to the truth and your destruction awaits as you drift further into your own ways. There is a way that seems right to a man, but the end thereof is death.

As I interact with my younger son, who is now 27, I realize the disadvantage children start with on the journey of life when a home is scattered. I feel God is in the healing process as he develops and prepares for the desire to be a dad and husband, but it has taken a focused effort even to this day to help restore and build his confidence in the right people, those who are positive and truly have his best interest at heart.

14. Three Stages of Hope and Success In The Development of A Loving Family

God is love...it is the attribute of divine being and purpose for creation to experience the wonder and mystery of life shared in fellowship and togetherness and given to man with the hope that he would realize the treasure of goodness and holiness in marriage until Jesus returns for his bride...the spotless church.

Love in its infancy is a dependant stage in which patterns and characteristics of the vulnerable individuals are shaped by the nurturing influences of a loving or Godly mother and father that has developed a spiritual depth of purpose and completeness together in obedience to an institution created by design for prosperity.

Similar in respect to the newborn child, the dynamics of marriage and the blending of the lifestyles of two uniquely different people require special attention that is too often presumptuously overlooked when the original parent of instruction and nourishment is naively disregarded as nonessential in the process of connection. Remember the reference, "and the two shall become one flesh." Our Father was giving us his instruction for the goal of marriage, a mystery in today's climate of divorce and infidelity, and blessing the union of a man and woman with physical fruit, that should remind spiritual, sensitive, caring, parents, of an unselfish mission of building a successful lineage. This ultimate goal or purpose as an institution established by God was to produce a Godly people and productive members within the family, and within society...a great nation... such as America was founded on. The two shall become one flesh, as the dynamics of cooperation and selflessness, (submission), attain a position of vulnerability of each member in the best interests of the group or nation developing and building trust, respect, reliability, reciprocity, and mutual benefits, vital in perpetuating validated, confidently strong individuals who feel safe, loved, valued, accepted or belonging to a productive thriving people. This training and development can only be maximized when two imperfect people through their accountability, and responsibility, to each other and in relationship with God is recognized and prioritized in harmony and love. Man's sin nature often creates challenges that can produce undesirable behavior in offspring even in the most spiritual environment... and for this reason alone, faith in an omniscient Creator becomes our only recourse when all else has seemed to fail, and ultimately, people refusing to mature in their individual responsibilities to the creator, family, and society, perpetuate a continuous element of rebellion and disregard for authority in the culture, and unless these patterns are broken by effective

E.V.M.

corrective discipline or a gift of divine intervention...the miracle known as salvation.

Stage One...

Boy meets girl, and love springs forth. Just as in the season of blossoms, as winter gives way to nature's revival of life. The lonely nights end as hibernating life stretches into its fullness of design. Excitement and adventure replace the routine, sleepy-eyed, listless day, and dreams and hopes come forward with anxious anticipation. Time shared passes so quickly, it seems months are only days and each waking moment brings with it one mission...to be with love again. It is too seldom understood that the romance, stimulating attractions that intensify emotional passions, found in first stage connection of the journey of the discovery experience of love potential, are in fact, "not love," but a natural sensation design of sexuality and human need for relationship placed in man by God. The eye knows what is pleasant to the stimulation of the minds mission of passion, but the reality of the inner person can cause a refocus of the initial image of first and early impressions, and the euphoria of the honeymoon phase to quickly give room to stage two. There are those certain experiences when we lose our balance and the ideal of romance is mistaken for committed love, often prematurely, and emotion investment becomes a risk to those who have deeper feelings than another. More frequently the male role withholds committed investment longer, and usually where sexual liberty is offered, individual value and appreciation is destroyed. For this reason individuals must protect their investment of their emotional self, "yes," including sexual intimacy with another, by not too anxiously or prematurely (before marriage), jumping into water that is too deep. The typical individual loses objectivity and discernment in a desperate effort to discover, capture, or recapture the excitement of love experiences, sometimes selfishly pursuing life sustenance in emotional moments of thrills and excited passions. Arriving at this position gives an unrealistic approach to life of ambitious greed and fantasies to immature individuals, preventing the ability to find contentment necessary to adjust to commitment. We are creatures of habit, and we establish patterns that can become mechanisms that become almost impossible to change even when we realize they are destructive appetites. Only God can give peace, joy, and love, with contentment. Without his spirit in the midst of hopeful relationships and obedience to his word, inevitable disaster is awaiting your dreams.

36

Stage Two...

Commitment is in fact a plan to" marry" a special individual that has been properly screened and proven trustworthy to sensitively handle another's emotions, protection, health, fragile ego, confidence, future plans and goals, investments, children, safety, stability, values, beliefs, ideals, desires, loyalty, purity, liberty, and submission, to accomplish a purpose of mutual success and benefits. Without marriage, there is no commitment because the ingredient of spirituality is ignored and because spirituality is an individual choice of belief systems we acknowledge as superior to natural physical necessity, each individual must consider the suitability of another's beliefs.

Commitment today seems to be a status to avoid...many people run in fear of historical traditional institutions...shouting ...failure, attempting to justify alternative lifestyles that are unscriptural. God created marriage just as everything he created perfectly and good and all he created still works, and is good. The common denominator in failure is man's choice to sin by disobedience. Most often the fear is that I will be stuck if I'm unhappy in marriage, so we approach life and relationships on every level except the most critical ingredient, commitment. If you're not happy, don't blame it on marriage, don't blame your spouse, don't blame Satan, you were happy when you made your choice."The problem is you." Commitment is the foundation of every relationship, starting with God, and commitment to Him means obedience to his ways. If we are unable to stay faithful to Him, we will never be able to stay faithful to any other, primarily because his spirit is a helper to lead, guide, and direct us through life and into all truth. Who would have imagined the boy or girl, who one short moment ago, drowning in love, has almost just as quickly, lost their excitement. God says he would give us the desires of our heart, if we delight in Him, not in man, woman, or possessions, how then without Him will we know what those desires are. It is impossible to know your heart with all the temptations and so-called options or alternative lifestyles of today. Any relationship attempting to build without God is certainly vain effort, yet we continue attempting to accomplish the impossible dream, without Him, being imperfect beings. A child is an amazing and wonderful example of commitment at its best and the results are clearly profound yet often quickly forgotten as greater challenges dim the recall of precious milestones of accomplishments. Remember baby's first steps? We never have to tell or even teach a child to walk, but his commitment to learn is observed visually as are many other patterns of development. More is caught...then is taught, so be sure your words match your actions or the observer will acquire a double standard until maturity allows correct value judgments. Success cannot be attained without ones commitment to the tasks necessary to accomplish the goal. It is a principle of reaping and sowing, and can be observed throughout life at every level and every attempt to achieve results, whether negative or positive, commitment to something will get you somewhere...prefer wise choices with positive results with promise and reward. Reaching the third and final stage of love is impossible without commitment, and for some reason, people fail because of a lack of integrity to promises.

Stage Three...

Love" returns," with reward. The children are raised and gone, the responsibilities are fewer, and the lessons of life have caused material desires to decrease with the realization that things are tools and have useful purpose, but they can't satisfy the inner needs we search to fill. Sacrifices no longer demand priority, and the pressures of interests outside the home can now be refreshing with freed up scheduling and proven trustworthiness in handling liberty. The interests or goals that were put on hold to nurture and develop young lives can be revived and creativity flourishes with experience and a deeper sense of an appreciation for the true important issues and treasures of life, and available time to address them adequately. Most people, due to the fast pace we live, never make it past stage one in relationships today, therefore they never experience the beauty of building an institution of stability and refuge, and the fulfillment and joy of a clear conscience, the safety and purity of faithfulness with a devoted spouse that has become your best friend, confidant, and inseparable companion. Many successful marriages would even comment of economic blessings rewarded to a mutual effort of diligently planning and building constructively and purposefully for this season of life. In the book of Ecclesiastes, King Solomon wrote that...the end of a thing is better than it's beginning...this being a principle of reward for faithfulness and commitment to the goals of marriage, and life, whether it be in your occupation, relationships, recreation, creativities or any task, the reward for diligence and patience will produce a pleasing gratification to those with pure hearts of purpose. Stewardship in our lifestyles faithfully committed to God will reward those who on that day will receive eternal life with Him, in heaven.

Therefore, let us slow our pace of life from the rushing freeways and city streets, and instant gratifications of foolish choices, that result in destruction, and begin to take the time to delight in a walk with God and His saints, taking time for family and friends that need our Christ-light, to give hope, in a dark, desperate, dying world...being committed to ...walking in love.

15. What Happens After Dad Has Gone?

One generation passeth away and another generation cometh. It is always the highest aim to prepare a child to become an individual empowered to strive forward on his own, to establish a legacy built on his own labors and rewards, and the privilege to participate in a season of co-existing in life's trials and pleasures, should be a normal experience for most families, but not necessarily does everyone move forward productively to build future generations of constructive experience. For several reasons, such as premature death, and divorce or perhaps an early inappropriate indiscretion, where life is conceived in sexual misconduct and responsibilities are misunderstood, the order of maturity has forced adjustments that can be suppressed for emotional desires or deep inner pursuits that push forward as significant confrontations for beliefs and values perceived by its victims unable to effectively meet demands of higher levels, without mentoring or wise counseling. Often the pain of lost hopes and dreams confused by tragic change in connecting links becomes a wall of fear to hide reality of difficult challenges when spiritual awareness is overlooked as a source to motivate overcoming adversity. Well, excuses are like opinions, everybody has one, and that's the nicest way I can express how I feel about a child born without a father's love invested in his well being or a mother who also fails to step up when we carelessly create patterns through irresponsible actions and attitudes. The bible says a man that doesn't provide for his own house is worst than an infidel (one who believes there is no God).

Directly addressing my own experience of divorce and the difficult and complicated adjustments required to restructure life and the strained relationship dynamics created within my family and with my own sons, I resolve one direction to take in fulfilling the responsibility of fatherhood and achieving maturity into manhood, and that is putting all your trust in seeking God in your life, and allowing him to direct you through the maze of this world's disorder and often seemingly overwhelming tasks at times, to equip you to meet the challenges of loving Him, and others, which includes your children, and yourself, after divorce has made you feel that you have failed in one of life's greatest pursuits or rejection has damaged emotions so severely, it seems all hope is lost. Remember, I can do all things through Christ, who strengthens me, and going it alone without people he will place in your path to help and support you or isolating yourself in shame and wounded ness, guarantees defeat, and destruction will become the ultimate result or legacy of inheritance you will leave behind for others to restore. God can fix it...with you or without you, for he is a help, comfort, deliverer,

39

redeemer, and friend to the innocent and heartbroken, and desires you to be whole and healthy physically, emotionally, and spiritually. Don't miss the blessings He has for you and your children, the joy restored, the pleasure refreshed, and the laughter renewed, will truly reveal to you the desires of your heart, when you delight your life in Him.

It intrigues me to realize when my own father died in 1979, I was a 29 year old father and husband with escalating issues in marriage, and as my oldest son and I share this book with you that we have compiled, mostly over the past year for me, he is in his 29th year of life and our relationship continues to flourish as I enjoy his family and look forward to sharing future blessings with my younger son and his family, not yet manifested. God has proven Himself faithful to me even as I face current issues of life, they never end until we die, and the hope of many years enjoying special days, they are truly every day, and the righteousness promised with walking with Him.

These thoughts I have shared won't happen by chance or coincidence, even with laborious efforts and attempts to build a solid foundation within your family...it can't be bought with money or attained with education...it can only be established through your faith in God.

16. A Natural Order to God's Design

How is it that in giving life, a woman experiences the closest brush with death that is known to man? At that moment, pain becomes a joy in bringing forth the child she has carried, suffering weeks, draining months, anticipating this one day, as a part of herself for nine months. How could she not be perfectly designed to nurture this new life, emotionally, and anatomically? This miracle a man can never experience in sweet agony, yet it is a creation of Gods order for a continuing cycle of mans existence, to perpetuate life, every single time a new life is presented.

God, however, created man anatomically to be stronger than woman for the labors of life as a provider and protector of those things that are weaker in endurance, thereby woman typically outlives man because of the emotional and physical duties required by life's continuous stress. His ability to be simple and task limited or focused, also reflects in detached resolution, sometimes required in life for very critical decisions, and for mundane experiences that must be made or lived out concerning the well-being of many. Man can stick to the task when the toil requires long-term involvement for survival, but often can get lost in his obligation for environment productivity, even at the expense of relational interaction. Man shall not live by bread alone, but by every word that proceeds from the mouth of God. To be fruitful and multiply, requires some developmental nurturing within emotional aspects of relational building providing for values of the individual and family purpose, being taught and instructed how to establish a heritage for future generations, to dwell together constructively. If a man is extremely sensitive, he may not be objectively decisive in decisions of life and death that may require instant reaction to threats, jeopardizing the whole group or mission. How many women could send their sons to war, if she knew eminently, he would die?

Yet, baring life is a gift to woman from God...a special arrangement of responsibility and wonder, given to the gender properly suited for his creative work, to direct nations morally and spiritually with sensitivity, tenderness, and gentleness of a God's love. How then, can a mother deny her natural intrinsic role or position within society as secondary or a homosexual presume to fulfill it fraudulently? A woman's role is primary, in fact, for the responsibility of first exposure to the world for every new life and the earliest development of a child...another compliment from God.

In nature that critical position is revealed strategically in place under the protection of the male species, even in lower forms of animal life. The female is the primary connection to the safety of the children because her role is multiplicity in conjunction with the male's role. If an enemy attacks the pack, the strong male by purpose is the first line of confrontation of defense. If he is a real male leader, his instinct will be to fight to the death if necessary to protect the female and children, as well as his position of authority. In the event he is defeated, first other strong males must step up to resume leadership, but in the case where this isn't possible, the female must then be the next line of defense for the infants, and in the animal kingdom, the combined force of the females instincts can be just as deadly to predators, and a foe weakened from battle with the male would hardly be a match for the female protectors. In the lion pride, the female is the hunter because the young must be provided for and she is well able to defend herself as a group with hunting skills, yet the male is the king, and his roaring will often ward off predators in warning to protect the young.

Have you ever observed the flocks of birds traveling long distance flying in columns with one bird at point to break the wind resistance, and as the lead fatigues, another will assume the point to resume flight while the others rest. " Are the little duckiest lined up in your journey of life, working together... to relieve pressures of resistance to building and sharing of responsibilities?"

Would a woman rather gracefully follow a strong man breaking a trail in the jungle or in the snow and wind or struggle to plow her own path through the elements of nature? Fatigued from a long journey a woman would be vulnerable to an enemies attack, being worn down by storms of life or society pressures. This is not hypothetical, but reality, a metaphorical example for our journey through. There are too many women unprotected physically and emotionally, often trying to pull along their children, and weak men (any man that won't work to provide for his family or anyone failing to commit to a woman he is living with, receiving the benefits of coexistence...but not sharing the responsibilities...that doesn't just mean contributing a little money), out of a subjective need for desires of passion that are real, yet unattainable to meet through shallow compromise of self-worth and precious values. Some women choose this dilemma...others don't understand, not having been instructed early in life by parents, which is everyone's responsibility, therefore they are not prudent in attitudes of life and seeking out information and truth. Fathers must teach their sons to be men, strong enough to endure the mundane task of repetitious labor, and sleepless nights of raising children, yet still sensitive enough to protect and care for the precious future by preparing them, and loving and sharing the duties along with the weaker vessel and must warn our daughters about predators disguised a societies solution to love and loneliness...whatever image they might be projecting.

CHP. 3   WHAT GOD REVEALS

17.   A Time And Purpose To Everything

I have found that the seasons of life come unpredictably in our journey through this world, but once arriving they make a definite, clear statement, concerning choices we have made, sometimes years earlier almost forgotten, and we are relegated to living out the harvest of those choices, whether positive or negative. I have heard it said and can relate to the fact that sex outside of marriage and commitment to that monogamous venture, inhibits our ability to focus on objective facts that truly should give precedence to how we decide our destiny. The pleasures of sex can prolong the agony of a bad relationship or marriage and prevent its victims from discovering more suitable partners as two people become lost in the confusion of emotional baggage and clear thinking becomes impossible, at best extremely difficult. The past is relative as an example of both good and bad choices, how we responded to their pressures, and an assessment of desired or undesired results. Many times we have compromised our values and principles to be involved with people that become our harsh correction to emotional vulnerabilities, which should mature us for future judgments, but too often we learn to love our poisons and ideal concepts of thing stat give us moments of pleasure and miss our opportunities for true happiness and peace...meantime, the clock is still ticking as time stops for nothing. Toxic lifestyles are real and the people that thrive on destructive existence, not considering the future, only living for the moment.

The bible says to live at peace with all men, as much as lies within you, leaving room for the fact it is impossible to get along with everyone. Another passage says, be angry, but don't sin...some Christians trying to unrealistically live without anger and even feel guilty when they allow moments of anger to rise, but everything, even anger, has its purpose when properly balanced and those who can't be confrontational can't resolve problems in interaction with people that can help us to understand others, even to recognize when it is a season or time for war. This world is imperfect, and evil or toxic philosophy must be met with appropriate resistance when its ominous presence lames over safety and peace.

I had a friend who was concerned with my anger towards my ex-wife as though I had not resolved my position with a woman who chose not to remain a part of my life after establishing family and obligations of responsibility. The past has certain reminders present in our future that tell us why we could not exist with someone we once believed we loved and submitted our safety, emotions, children, and well-being to. This past Christmas my sons and granddaughters spent the day with the ex. She had a new boyfriend that joined in with my family, while I spent the day with my brother and his family. Ironically, a few weeks later she had another new boyfriend and arrogantly stated, "I've been known to get rid of a man at the drop of a hat." Well, that's one more holiday divorce robbed from us and a stranger passing through enjoyed the experience that he had no investment in the lives that were celebrating. As we establish patterns we are also building habits in how we relate to life, and the abnormal is accepted as normal.

Microwave relationships are like a freeway, some travel faster than others, in the wrong lanes, and someone is getting on, while others are getting off. Needless to say, the next relationship has terminated, nothing to brag about, nothing valuable learned, just put on a facade everything's ok, just another commute in the journey of life. Do you think we remember heavily traveled roads need a lot of repair and maintenance? The bible tells us not to be anxious for anything, not even the good and pleasant things life offers, for there is a price to be paid in some form for everything we do. I hadn't heard from my son and daughter-in-law for the 4th of July, but the next evening I was informed my grandbabies had been in town for the holiday weekend with the ex...do you think it strange that I was not contacted...seems almost deliberate that the woman who walked away so long ago and continues to expose my children to questionable characters, but the past reminds me why I don't like her actions and behavior patterns that cover what perhaps is pain of the reality of consequences, maybe even shame...but the truth can hurt, and the next generation is infected with disharmony and separation before their innocence blooms to flourish in the issues of life...the abnormal, becomes normal.

I had to hurry home to keep my thoughts fresh and with you being so busy at work, I knew the opportunity to speak to you was limited, as usual, but everything has a reason or purpose. As I overheard you discussing going to workout with your friend, I couldn't help but think how lucky he is to spend time with you. Now that you have exposed your intellect and ability to convey deep thoughts of life, I long to share other experiences to understand your feelings and perspective on things that matter. I'm sure you know I will always respect a person's choice to spend time with whomever they chose to, it's just the way you carry your attitudes and your mental qualities that intrigues me. I have always carried the belief that when I meet someone like you, if the opportunity is not available to build a closer relationship, then I continue to look forward to that special woman who will make the time available, and it helps me to realize how even more special she must be. In discussing my offer to help you with female friends, they said I needed to tell you that my offer did not come with a condition or expectation. It seemed for a few days that you questioned my intent, but you must have resolved your question, my own observation of reactions of recent visits, feel free to correct me if not. You are a wonderful person, very special to me. Sometimes small things people do can mean more than you can quite understand, and I know how difficult things may be in our struggles and issues of life, but like I previously stated, life is made up of choices and beliefs and how we respond, determines our character. Thank you frie-nnnnnd, "smile", kind of a joke, for being so sweet, receptive, and affectionate, because you didn't have to be. I know no one is perfect as we try to understand as we live and God reveals to us what we need to know, at the proper time.

I was offering to a mutual friend the opportunity for his group to perform at an outdoor revival, but he didn't feel ready, and said he didn't want to send people the wrong message. The bible says that all have sinned, and I haven't always been a Christian...but everyone must start at the beginning and be in the process of maturing in God's word. A wise elder in my church once said this..."wherever good is, evil is also present", and that really helped me to understand spiritual warfare better, my purpose as a believer, the people I interact with, and I can then picture myself in a mirror after I have made a mistake. I am just a man in my flesh, but those needs are also real, but we must do things God's way, if we desire to live in his blessings.

It would be a facade for a man to act as though he didn't need to or want to hold a beautiful woman in his arms, but it is also wonderful to hold her first in your heart and share her mind, emotions, and spirit, which is a gift from God. In the book of Proverbs it states that a prudent wife is from God, therefore such a woman is worth waiting for. Sometimes I wonder if you recall the things I share in thoughts because you seldom comment in response to conversations or things I share in writings, but I have recognized, most people don't know how to respond, meaning perhaps a fear of intimacy or unwillingness, but this thought I hope you will always remember. We move through this life and our society has deceived us into thinking that the good things in life are enough to satisfy, and we stumble while building relationships we were created for. We seek after good jobs, friends, cars, homes, hope for a good marriage and everything our ideals can imagine. God even gifted us with built in radar, talent, physical attractiveness that appeals to the interests of others instinctively. Call it karma or familiar spirits, everybody's looking for a soul mate. The bible urges us first to seek the kingdom of heaven, and promises all these things will be added as we are preparing for the responsibilities and accountabilities of faithful stewardship to God that he expects as he blesses us with good things. As we learn to trust him, not ourselves, we don't know enough, we learn to be patient and wait for his best which surpasses just good, and with his guidance our hearts desires are meet, that we can not understand because we live in a world of temptation. Temptations are never from God, but from the evil in our hearts through lusts, jealousy, envy, and hate, and let us realize we are children of Satan when we yield to selfish desires. God says he will always provide a way of escape from temptation, for those who really love him and want to obey his commandments. In our imperfect understanding we do make mistakes so often forgetting that God does test and try us to build our character and faithfulness, but we do not practice or participate in willful sins that move us away and separates us from his will for us. They that wait upon the Lord shall renew their strength, they shall mount up on wings as an eagle, they will run and not be weary, and they shall walk and not faint. Is. 40:31.

God's love

18. Created For Prosperity

God gave Adam, the first human of creation, instructions to follow to live out man's eternal life with purpose to be productive and enjoy the wonders of earth and the heavens, in harmony with nature and perfect spiritual relationship with him in the midst of a geographical garden of paradise designed for creator and creation to communicate love for his glorious plans for life. With singleness of mind, Adam obediently trusted God and the blessings of splendor were his to enjoy completely in the pleasures of God's presence. And everything God created, he said that it was good, and yet his infinite compassion and complete understanding of relationship had a plan for something more. God knew that it was not good for man to be alone, and his hope for his creation to fill the earth with life and purpose, just as he had filled the heavens with wondrous life of celestial design, he began to unfold, when he created woman. He wanted man to have something he could touch and embrace to experience his wonder of pleasure in emotions of the eye, the mind, and body to bring laughter, passion, caring, and children along with a high esteem for his love. He created man and woman in his image and gave them the gift of life to produce life that he creates even to this day, every time a child is born.

Eve, the first woman, created with the attributes of God, just as man, for both natures are within him, not distinct within creation of woman as some would suppose, was created to help Adam in the plan for the future, a marvelous gift to life called marriage, not sex. Sex is the method for reproduction and pleasure within the commitment of marriage, and its purpose is corrupted in all other forms of involvement, because it is designed with protection for the emotions and health, mental and physical, of a family unit that includes the well being of children and a prosperous future of productive growth to establish nations.

The truth of creation is we were designed to glorify God by obedience and reverence but man alone has fallen to disobedient living while all of nature remains faithful to God in doing his will. The sun, moon and stars obey, the animal kingdom continues to obey, and time, as we know it remains, until God intervenes at his appointed time. The serpent deceived the woman. He took the truth and twisted it, and in her desire to increase in wisdom, she compromised her position in authority and God punished her with pain in childbearing and by placing her desire for her husband. Woman is still attempting to reestablish her order of authority and desire taken as punishment for sin and the struggle to usurp correction blemishes her ability to submit to leadership. Because she compromised through listening to the subtle voice of a liar, women today are sill seduced by voices not having their best interest in mind. Satan's plan of divide and conquer has produced disastrous affects through out time and the battle of the sexes continues as men blame women and women blame men and neither submit to the authority of God's spirit. Adam loved Eve, and could have protected her if he had obeyed God's instructions to him, instead, he listened to the urge's of his wife to eat the forbidden fruit, partaking in disobedience with knowledge of error, and as it remains today, men know what they should be doing as leaders in the home, community, and church, they just won't do what's right being tempted by every distraction imaginable. Man of his own free will disobeys God, and the calamity of sin receives its reward of destruction and death. God today, still holds man accountable to him, regardless of societies trends, even though woman was first partaker in sin.

19. Do We Always Have To Know, Why?

There was a time in my life I wouldn't have openly shared these thoughts with anyone, even if I knew their affections towards me were sincerely felt, in a special way. I would withhold my true feelings of inner expressions exposing what I knew were my real desires. Maybe that's just the man in me who's pride wouldn't reveal his vulnerability or perhaps, his unwillingness to be honest enough to tell a woman how unique she is, refusing to give her what she deserves in knowing how lovely she truly is, in fear of her walking away into the arms of another man, with a confidence in understanding she is loved. Somehow I knew this experience was supposed to be related to a daughter by her father first, but you see how we so often hide behind emotional walls of fear, not knowing the heart of someone we want to be closer to intimately. This journey of life can leave you puzzled if you selfishly hold on to true feelings, and sincere compliments we need to risk sharing, that can build someone up, when life so often, has brought many down to insecure fears that leave us timid and weak to rejection that so often is bad timing or life issues unconsciously misunderstood through inexperience. Today, I feel I know myself, and wish that this were how everyone could feel ...in knowing our heavenly Father's love is all the assurance we need.

They say a girl always looks for something in a man her father early in childhood development brings out, in her search to know, she is lovely. If her dad was a wonderful nurturing man, she tries to repeat the experience with the man she meets to consider her future life of bliss, and if he was neglectful in building her confidence, she tries to replace him, in deep inner feelings of desire and is mysteriously drawn to men like him in an attempt to find what has always been missing in the dreams of a little girl, still remaining to be cherished by that male enigma. We can search a lifetime, acting out that inner need in romantic escapades, lured in by this desire of wanting to feel we're loved, as though it were an emotion we can turn on and off to fit interests or attractions at convenient moments, overlooking or missing the fact that first you must know God's love for you and his purpose that reveals your value and worth to this life. Young men and women still flocking to the night spots looking for the right person, only to discover, eventually for the wise, hopefully for others," that you have to become the right person", while in the moments that are stolen in deceit and pretense, we miss many opportunities in sharing true feelings of intimacy in sharing love, found on time...in God's will. Problem is, that old nature of flesh, me man, you woman, and people really believe it is so simple, thinking things will somehow work out in the end, not recognizing need for assessment of character needed for " long term stability everyone wants." So many women, all ages, swept off their feet by an aggressive, good looking, young, prospect, eagerly waiting to speak soft words in her ear...of things she wants to believe," not necessarily the truth", and she falls into the dilemma of objectivity lost, giving her most precious gift of her inner spirit to a man, so easily, instead of a God who wants her to have the desires of her heart. Boys and girls still play games and passions run free, until the need for more than sex and romance surfaces, sometimes in the form of a newborn, and you discover "babies daddy", was just playing a game. In 1965, children born out of marriage was at a 20% rate in the Black culture in America, and in 2004, it has literally reversed to 80% born to unwed mothers. Caveman mentality always comes up short when baby needs pampers and milk, reality...if we would only look ahead, responsibilities of life are to demanding for productive people to hang with the crowd too long, remaining unconstructive, and not counting the cost for pleasure.

It would be so easy to say how a first look creates such a strong desire of curiosity to know the deep thoughts of a beautiful woman, and hopes to share adventurously exciting moments of quivering embraces with her... loves mystery revealed when looking deeply into her eyes, feeling lost in enchantment. Long wet. Kisses of refreshing waters. Her mouth is warm, smooth, sweet with nectar, as she entices my parting lips to tenderly kiss her lips, moist and separated...her touch speaks invitation, hands so soft, as they curiously wonder in anatomy investigation...tan skin, supple with oils of fragrant lotions...her flawless hair falling down below her petite shoulders, revealing prepared care in pleasing her man's desire...even in the statuesque beauty of her eloquent neck as I brush her hair gently aside, pulling her closer to smell her perfume merging with natural juices, arousing my nature with her moist skins anticipation, my control, my strength is bursting and I can feel her breath as her heart beat rises...our clothes have become a nuisance... she invites me to kiss her again, softly... softly...she softly... whispers with her kisses as she says my name, Errol... make love to me...just to speak her thoughts, knowing we had no choice... understanding now in quiet moments of silent, gentle, moaning... then emotions speak in realizing thoughts available only in the words, baby, I love you... for her, as we hold each other entwined in body and mind...

As sleep eventually overtakes our exhausted apex but passions refuse to let her sweet, wet, body go...and in our purpose, the bliss of pleasures fulfilled mission, morning arrives.

Her laughter I hear from a distance, and her smile so enchanting...every moment possible...spent together. Hand in hand, walking on the seashore... dancing slowly, holding her closely...together,

To watch the sun go down in the hues of reds and yellows stretched across the sky...yesterday...dreams of golden sunlight of morning, its promise and trust in knowing love...a new beginning has been discovered. Who is she? Is this just a dream? Only fantasy? She can only be my wife... for I could not trust another with my heart, my mind, my soul...my love is for you alone.

For years, I have searched to give my gift of love away, but did not know that, first I must find it in God, only his overflowing love in me could give it away and still have an abundant supply remaining for others. Our world is moving so fast and is so impatient...people rushing forward, hasty to know, and trying to understand what they are searching for... it all seems so elusive, our efforts often fail. Life has brought me to its horizon, learning to trust God, instead of my own desires. It hasn't been easy, but I continue growing and the potentials of the future are exciting. Your gentleness and warmth have touched and awakened me and I can say it feels good to be free to express what living means. Yes, I loved your dimples, from the moment I first saw you, and yes, I have wanted to kiss your lips when your face so softly presses to mine in innocent affection, but I have learned to truly know a woman, she must be willing to give you her time. We always make time in life for what we feel important. Can a man love a woman from a distance? It is so difficult, but we've learned love is unconditional, realizing this is an imperfect world, and patience truly is a virtue.

We make a huge mistake not trusting God, even fall in love with the wrong people, but He can take our mistakes and work them out for the good, that's what forgiveness is all about. Our world is full of brokenhearted people that Jesus came to restore their hope. Love knows no color, race, or age, and yet it knows its borders...It is kind, patient, and alive. "God is love." It is precious and wonderful when it is shared in truth and honesty. Can you catch a falling star and make a wish come true...or trust God and make a dream...reality.

20. Give Me Liberty or Give Me Death

Liberty... is where freedom is enjoyed with choice of actions taken, and lived out, and wholesome behavior is the product of truth and pure experiences of life. But guilt, produced by destructive moral choices, steals liberty and converts it to bondage, even when the activity involves pleasures...we know established moral boundary's are engrained in everyone except those with a seared conscience, and once the erroneous patterns are exposed to others, manifesting truth of character...shame is born, often a major effort to conceal the truth of reality of unacceptable behavior is birth, (deception, lying), and freedom becomes feelings of unworthiness, dangerously increasing value disorder and negative attitudes of compromised purpose, and the loss of spiritual direction ensnares you in lifestyles of death to enlightenment to creative freshness of joyful living we are given by a loving Creator, every single day. Living out of control creates a perversion of dynamics and individuals consumed in undisciplined behavior obsessively attempts to control others within their influence in a useless design to redefine order or tyrannical controlling. The freedom to love with liberty and fullness of joy with peace of mind and contentment is destroyed as trust issues escalate within the structure of established accountabilities to others, and often the atmosphere created in fraud will abort the security and confidence in relationships, and identities are distorted or lost in quandary. Participants and observer's can only inquire in speculation..."what happened."

In many ways in my life, especially in my years of marriage, I have tried to show others their value, not just to me, but most importantly, how they see themselves. Did you know that it is impossible to make someone who chooses to be miserable...happy? If you are not careful in attempts to understand and focus all attentions in discovering resolution to toxic people and their patterns, you can actually lose your own identity in failing to nurture and mature the one person that adjustments and developments that can be experienced in evolving processes of life...you. Have you ever noticed how the innocent child plays and laughs with everyone openly and freely, until their pure world is contaminated with adult ideals and practices a child can't understand? Even when the old, who have slowed from the fast pace of life have burned the candle of pleasures, they return to a life of purity and simplicity because exposure to pollutants once again is minimized due to inactivity, but still some remain young at heart...or is it dirty old person?

Not necessarily true for everyone, but often constructed walls that shield from the pain experienced in the liberty of choices made in youth...

gone wrong, and a problem of the old who are no longer flexible and giving like the child, but have become rigid, and adventure is lost to fears as the unknown is simply avoided even when it can be something good. That's why they say you can't teach an old dog, a new trick.

Many people fail to see the responsibility that comes with freedom, not considering the inevitable consequences of choices made too quickly or underestimating the consequences, becoming consumed in pursuing passions, failing to realize others will enjoy the seasons of fun, but not the work it takes to build a trusting and lasting relationship. The whole theme of Jesus' life was in putting the concerns of others first, not in seeking his own selfish interests or desires, and in the big picture he was willing to die for us as a pardon for our sins. People so cunningly conceal their motives until the bait is taken, then the heart of a man is revealed in his integrity to his commitments. Jesus is my pattern for life and my motives I try to keep open for examination, but people, my past imperfections, and my desire to enjoy sharing life with others sometimes makes it difficult not to become disappointed with this life...but not my hope of eternal life he made possible to us.

Spiritual warfare is real in our lives as we exist in this horizontal relation to each other, and when we fail to involve God, who is vertical in relation to us, we are going to fail repeatedly, and pride prohibits us from humility as our anger blames others for what we permit to happen to us, and instead of needed change we perpetuate mistakes not recognizing only God can give us the wisdom and strength to fight our lustful desires once we have opened our spirit to their pleasures. A former homosexual male having become a converted believer, now married with children, but yet struggling with his attractions to other men, even though he no longer desires his former lifestyle, reveals the dangers and consequences we don't consider when passions of desire is ruling our thoughts. The struggle must be won in the mind first if the victory over the battle is to become permanently fixed in repentance. One important fact we fail to acknowledge in idealistic thinking, and so-called moral majority or new age philosophy of popular acceptance is that man's potentials of great accomplishment. Talents, and gifts can be used for" great evil," just as well as for much good. Who was Hitler...who killed Jesus...what motivates Jihad...does marriage promote abortion, or the experimental use of sex without commitment, does exploration of the vast universe at the expense of billions of dollars wasted, while people are starving, homeless, and dying impress victims of need, does a lifestyle of liberal morality that is disease rampant validate individual rights of choice? Who cares who won the Super Bowl last year or who is sleeping with whom in Hollywood, when a loved one is dying?

Did you know it is more important that two people have the same faith than it is to be the same race, even with all our cultural differences? How can darkness and light dwell together? It is impossible in the long haul, yet we continue to try, not knowing the future, and who the true believers of God are in this earth realm, while Satan is continually deceiving, and the spirit of antichrist is everywhere and in everything we experience on earth. But fear is not from God, but rather liberty "with" truth. He promises us abundant life while we live here, but we continue to choose to live below the privilege we have as Christians. Yes, we do experience the same circumstances as non-believers, but we are promised the wings to soar above the problems of life, walking in fellowship with Jesus and others who believe. How much evidence is needed that "for God so loved the world, and all its inhabitants, that he gave his only begotten son, that whosoever believes in him should not parish, but receive everlasting life," giving opportunity of choice that " none would parish, but that all would come to the knowledge of the truth," and his wisdom allows those who "truly... truly love Him" to remain a part of this sinful world experience as a light of hope for those who are still in darkness. People would dare to question his omnipotence, failing to realize if eternity were left in the hands of man, we would have fear of a nuclear holocaust. We somehow believe we are going to live this conscious life experience forever as we understand it now, and that is so foolish to presume as we compromise the future for immediate gratifications because they can be reached easily, only to discover we sold our soul to Satan, and never recognized the deal we were making. Count the costs before you make your choices because once they are made, the consequences will surely follow. Jesus may very well be the only friend still there...when all the others have left you alone... to fight your struggles.

21. Home of The Free?

Escape in Iraq...the Thomas Hamill Story,

Listening to his experience as a truck driver caring fuel for military transportation in a war zone, it reminded me of the two lane roads I frequently traveled as a 20 year old in Viet Nam. The difference in 33 years, is that in Iraq you can also find 6 lane freeways full of fast pace travel and convoys with a dozen or two big rigs escorted by military firepower. He described points called "kill Zones", that could be the length of a football field, but instead of a contest, death was there and this day he had to face it, and being independent in his actions, he only had God to rely on. The bullets sounded like golf balls penetrating the metal of the trailer, and as he looked in front and behind, he could hear and see the exploding trucks hit by fire, then suddenly a round sheered through his cabin and turned to shrapmetal penetrating his forearm and gorging his flesh deeply and shattering the bone. He began praying as he wrapped a tourniquet around the pumping blood as the insurgents captured him, first on camera to us as propaganda, with the threat of decapitation, then as they took him to a building and barricaded him in an armed-guarded room. He began repeating the 23rd Psalms...yea though I walk through the valley of the shadows of death, and somehow on the 24th day, hearing the thunder of approaching trucks, a military convoy, he rushed to the door, knowing his opportunity for escape had come. Amazingly as he fled, the guard who only 15 minutes earlier stood at the door was not there to resist his escape, and as the reserve unit searched the area around the building, they found an abandoned AK-47 laying on the ground. Their mission for the day was to locate a busted pipeline, not to rescue Thomas, but God put the convoy in the right place to deliver his child. Thomas Hamill is a third generation farmer in the southern states, who was facing losing his farm, and had gone to Iraq to work in an effort to save his inheritance from his father and his grandfather.

The doctor that performed his surgery shared a story of how Sadam Hussien had a vaccine that could have saved millions of lives of children in Iraq, but he refused to use it allowing them to die, to use their deaths as propaganda against the U.S., and people still feel we should not be there to free these people who have been lied to and prevented access to media to hear the whole story, but only allowed to see what Sadam's regime wanted to indoctrinated them to believe.

Remember 9-11, people kill the innocent when they are polluted in thinking they have a cause...Bin Laden has been reduced to that last video he made...if he could have delivered his threats he would have done so in the name of Jihad. We live in America with all the luxury and safety life can offer, and would dare to oppose a God fearing president like George Bush, a man of divine appointment for such a time as this, and as young Americans and Allies are giving their lives around the world for what they believe is justice and truth, we protest at ease because of the freedom of speech, and rights of belief.

As the death toll rises in Iraq, consider this...every year, around the world in countries where the Muslim faith and other false religions control its people by force and fear of death and torture, the death toll of Christians killed for their faith in God is approximately 160,000 lives each year. Do we hear these statistics in the news media that is worldwide? Does our government wait until our liberty is threatened on our soil to oppose evil terrorism?

Wake up people...while there is still time to save freedom for our children. The reports of finding no weapons of mass destruction by the U.N. task teams, does not overshadow the numerous mass grave sites discovered under roads and attempts to conceal the murder of innocent men, women, and children in Iraq, and their torture for the right and freedom to believe the truth.

22. Worship

I worship God because
He gave me dreams as a young man
And gifts to pursue them...
He protected me from danger
Under my parents covering
And as a young man in Viet Nam.
He blessed me with sons
And not having daughters by birth
He has given me many daughters
To treasure
And share the experience of life...
He allowed me to watch my sons
Become men
And though Satan tried
To steal my joy of fatherhood
He...would not allow him
To succeed
Though dead in my sins
He...has proven His faithfulness
Time and time again..
He...healed my mind
And my body,
From infirmities
And restored my hopes for the future
And my joy for daily living...
He...has given me
The abundant life
His word has promised
And I am walking
In His garden of delight...
Though many friends
Have failed me...
And in my imperfection
I also failed them,
But He has never left...
Or forsaken me...
His salvation is
My lifeblood,

Without worship
I could not know His love,
Nor, could I adore Him...
He is perfecting
His love in me,
So that
He...can reach others
Through me...
He comforts me
in knowing...
I can come to Him
when this world has
discouraged me...
And He,
is always available...
though weeping has endured many
nights,
His joy
finds me...
in the morning...
His word...
refreshes me...
when I am tired,
and his spirit...
renews me,
when I struggle and fail,
and condemnation...
is overcome.
in worshipping Him,
His love draws me,
closer to my purpose, my hope,
and my destiny...
worship is preparing me
for my eternity
with Him.
Worship is
paying homage to God,
a holy, superior being,
who is

divine perfection...
it is preaching, reading of the scrip-
tures,
singing, praying, giving alms, bap-
tism,
and communion,
ultimately
it is obedience to a deity
reverence and honor to
His omnipotence...
whether in the midst of the congre-
gation,
or when I am
all alone...
worship takes my concerns
from the cares, worries, fears and
frustrations
of this world
and puts my focus
On God
And His perfect will
For my life
Eternally and currently...
I then can rise to my feet
In recognizing in a prostrate state
Of humbleness
To Him
That He is God;
In Heaven
And I am
His creation
A man of little understanding
And few needs other than those
He generously provides...
His people of the nations
Have been deceived
By the works of the evil one
And their discernment of spiritual
things
Has vanished
Because they honor man and pos-
sessions
And fail to realize the need
To honor, praise, and worship
Him...
They all chase after illusions,
And His kindness and presence
Is far from them,
But their desire for greed
Has destroyed their success...
They think they sleep safely
In their houses
And their bellies are full
Of the deceitfulness
Of this world,
But their prosperity
Will not last
And their families and children
Will suffer
Because they have rejected
The truth of his precepts
For the comforts of the moment,
And his desire to bless them
Has turned to curses
For rejection of fellowship with
Him
In worship.
Worship is like a great door
And Jesus
Is the keeper of the door...
who then can enter into that door
without knowing who He is
that watches those who are entering
certainly there are many doors,
but how will they know
the right door
without worship.
every man is aiming for a mark
he draws the bow and aims his ar-
row
towards the target
but how will he hit the mark

without the proper projection, practice, and training
without first learning
the techniques of success
from a teacher,
one learned in experience
to endure the elements of opposition
to the goal.
it would compare to a newborn
child
attempting to fly an airplane
he cannot understand
the instruments or gauges
he has not grown
to maneuver flight controls
he must first be allowed to mature
and be ready to learn
to experience success and failures
then return to study
and meditate on the task
for understanding
to again approach the target

with acquired skills and confidence
he has attained in purpose and support
He has done that which was necessary
He can meet the challenges ahead...
this can be perfected
only through worship
the stabilizing factor
we must recognize
it balances the variables of living
in this complicated world
of temptations and distractions
successfully overcoming
Through the spirit of God
working in us
to confront the evil of today
walking with our redeemer?
In worship.

23. Unconditional Love

We had just finished the night shift and the usual spurts of conversation had not been possible during the night, maybe it was by design, I don't know, but the story I was about to hear left me anxious to rush home to the keyboard to capture the message planted in my mind and in my future hopes for meeting someone to share an unconditional love. My first impressions had been polluted by gossip I had not requested from co-workers, reflecting a young woman employed with our company that I had only had brief encounters with. Now circumstances had placed her on our shift, and the opportunity to know her became almost inevitable as the interaction presented a new picture of the attractive young woman through conversations we began sharing about our lives. She had recently married a very humble young man on another shift and the buzz in the building was full blossom question and doubt of proper planning and thinking involved in this complicated decision chosen in union. You see, she had just had a baby by another man, someone who had left her hanging and hurting in despair. She had already shared with me that she had vowed to God that she would not mess up again, and being pregnant, and abandoned, her anger, bitterness, and frustration, had left her broken and disillusioned. The young husband was a friend of hers who had watched her, admired her, and fallen in love with her beauty, and his captivation watched her go through the bad experiences in the previous relationship, but his compassion and unconditional love world not allow him to turn his back on the wounds of his friend, even though he had not revealed his growing affections as he was overlooked by the young woman in favor of the relationship with the father of the newborn. His admirable response to her broken spirit was that of a rescuer, the knight in shining armor fearlessly confronting fears and selfish pride, to proclaim his deep conviction of increasing love..." I lost you once, I won't lose you again." Was this a decision of foolishness and inexperience or a lesson in passion and forgiveness? All my thoughts could conclude was that in today's world and lifestyles of change and unfaithfulness, this quality was unusual and selfless.

It is interesting to note that the newlyweds had been developing the relationship only as a friendship, long before the mistake had taken place in trusting the babies daddy, and the unforeseen pregnancy that resulted, once disclosed openly, had left the friend and future husband, not contemplated, crushed and discouraged, but somehow, his love did not die. It seems the strength displayed by these two young people has a certain testimony of never giving up even when you know your own bad choices have brought negative and painful consequences and difficult situations to challenge.

The young woman was no stranger to adversity, having been emotionally abandoned from the age of 15, and forced to conduct life making mature choices she was not yet equipped to master, and forced to fight for everything she had attained in life. With two children by a previous relationship she had been forced to terminate upon discovering the use of crack cocaine, and an abusive fiend attempting to control and force his behavior on her and the children, forcing her to find the strength to walk away to live and struggle to retain dignity, often working two jobs to provide for the needs of her children.

Now, the newlyweds have taken on the task of legally adopting her children, while the natural father of the newborn has relinquished his rights to forego paying child support, and they are working together in submission to each other, while they focus on ways to keep the fire burning, while working through complicated schedules and adjustments to daily issues of living.

We go through horrific trials in this life, but when you hear a story like theirs, it sets a level of standard very high in forgiveness, sharing, communication, compassion, and love that tells us to never give up on dreams and goals, even when this imperfect world has clouded ideals we conceive. Keep believing and trust in God, and all things are possible. When life has given you a lemon...make lemonade! Your bright future doesn't know anything about the past mistakes, and God is a God of new beginnings. Humility is a valuable lesson to learn, but God is far form those who are proud and self-exalting. Didn't Jesus humble himself and die an embarrassing death on the cross for our sins, and we all have committed some serious offenses, but he made it possible for forgiveness to bring new life, new hope, and an eternal future.

Everything logical would tell us the odds for this young couple today is not good in a selfish, me centered society, and pessimism would say they won't make it...but what is important is they believe that they can, against all odds, and just maybe they will.

Did you know that with God on your side, even all alone...the odds are in your favor when you trust Him...even if everything else is against you?

24. Somebody's Got to Submit

I first had to decide if I wanted to share this information, realizing the selfishness we are all capable of as created beings, but as I assess the potential of affecting others in a positive way, I feel free to do the right thing. As I build my thoughts in presentation I realize my organization might be random to some. That just means we are on a different pages, and that's still ok, because no one is perfect, and if we had been able to collaborate on this book, the message God is trying to tell us is, "we move closer to understanding solutions." Now that I've said that, write your book and allow the purpose of your creativity to touch the life of someone in a provocative message of hope and connection. Many people fail to realize, in an instant, we impact other people and add to the construction of building up or tearing down of lives. The difference between a smile and an angry outburst of road rage can affect today, which is all that we are promised, and if we can't effectively process what happens in our deep inner or subconscious man, our spirit is stamped with negative emotion, and a stockpile of negativity continues to grow. If we are blessed to see tomorrow, be thankful for the miracle that has happened, that one thing alone should be enough to propel you forward with joy and anticipation, and if someone else is raining on your parade, get an umbrella or get out of the rain. Jesus Christ is an umbrella. He said, "if you continue in my word, then are ye my disciples indeed; and ye will know the truth, and the truth will make you free." John 8:31,32. Many people have said they have tried that church thing and it don't work, so they stop remembering God on Sunday and expect their lives to prosper constructively by coincidence, doing anything and everything that pleases self and forget Jesus is God, and he is omniscient and you would dare to say the truth doesn't work. Realizing 7 days a week the world is bombarding every living soul on this planet with pollution, and contamination is spreading in our lives as well as in nature, and you are asking God for a sign so that you can believe he is real? There is no hope outside of Jesus and Sunday alone is not enough to contend with spiritual contamination, just because you went to church. You better wake up and take the garbage you can smell out of your house (mind, spirit), so that you can enjoy the good food (God's word), that can nourish you back to health and strength, that you might begin to heal others and enjoy the fresh air of freedom. It's not all about me...it's not just about you either.

I would like to thank God, first of all, but realizing others before me also had to hear God's message of love and truth, then sacrificially share and send it down through the generations of our ancestors, both paternally and maternally, reaching to me and my siblings to allow today, a greater opportunity for life and the promises we wait for. I also would like to thank my son Errol Jr. who has collaborated and coauthored this book, for his insight and action, my son Terrell for his inspiration and confidence, and my ex-wife, Denise, for giving birth to my blessings that have motivated my hope and drive, when I was ready to give up. Matt, by brother and pastor, for his leadership and trust, and my sisters that have been there always to support me, even in the early foolish days of our lives, when we did not understand, and Cenne', Mariya, and Minyon, who give me joy, laughter, and love. Tamara, a friend who supported me when I was emotionally sick, and Jasmine, Tiffany, and J.J., that showed love and strength in my weakness, and all those beautiful children that laugh and play and help me to remember.

Errol Sr.

25. What Monsters Are Alive In Your Life

Most people approach life as though it were an experiment instead of an adventure. The problem existing in this attitude is this...experiments exceed limits and desired results and actual results will more often than not vary. Frankenstein was an attempt by a doctor to create life, but the unpredictable factors resulted in an uncontrollable force of fear, death, and destruction, and no way to assess who is in harms way. The common nature of pain is to turn on the source or creator of that pain or man's rage and hurt, turning on self or fellow man in a misguided path or pattern. The difference in the purpose of an adventure is in the elements of known factors. You know where you are headed, when you are leaving, the distance of your destination, what you need to accomplish on the journey, the approximate time involved, and the people affected by the mission. In trusting God, we also know who made the adventure possible and why the journey was necessary. Excluding God relegates your journey to only what you can provide with all its limitations and diminishes your adventure to a routine experience with no lasting excitement, no hope, no anticipation, no purpose, and finally, no joy. The bible is a road map of life to those who are going somewhere and can guarantee success to anyone who follows its course of direction. Without its guide, you can not experience the adventure God promises for your purpose, but there is a guarantee your experiment will leave you with consequences you didn't desire and an eternal parting from the adventure and reward of believing in the truth of God's word by faith in trusting him. Sadly we observe the lives of others as though they are barometers for what we choose to believe, and this deception distracts us from the perceptions of the best for your life. God is always dealing with us uniquely in a personal relationship and corporately only as we stand together in harmony, agreement, and peace, by his power. A barometer can tell what the conditions are outside, but they cannot control or predict perfectly the variables of nature's changes from hour to hour or what tomorrow may bring.

Just as it is easier to see in the distance what lays ahead on a clear spring morning, rather than stumbling in the darkness of night or when storm clouds have made moving ahead impossible, sin in our lives separates us from God's best and we become vulnerable to the limited wisdom we have only in the experience of trial and error, but experimenting with the forces of nature can produce dangerous and deadly results. What happens when you are facing an obstacle never before confronted in life? Where do you turn and what information do you seek to guide you through the unknown? King David's example shows how being out of position with God leaves us open to sin and tragedy. In every challenge prior to his staying behind in Jerusalem while his men were at battle, God was with him. His failure to lead his men, being in his proper position, led to his adultery with Bath Sheba, the murder of Urea, her husband, in an attempt to conceal his sin, her pregnancy, and death of the child she bare with him. David took his eyes off God and had the fighting men of Israel counted, reflecting the military strength of Israel instead of God's power, which angered God and opened the way for Satan, never before refered to in battle against Israel and allowed him to come against God's people. His leadership as a father faultered in effectiveness resulting in consequences his own children suffered as a direct result. His daughter Tamar was raped by her brother Amnon, right under his nose, which lead to his son Absalom's despise and rebellion of him, the vengeance reflecting the killing of Amnon by Absalom, and the eventual conflict of rule of the kingdom, which led to Absalom's murder by Joab, against the kings orders. Again God's anger sent plagues and even an angel of the Lord against the people because of the king's sin. Yet still, God is faithful, and a repentant David, though not allowed to build a temple to the Lord himself, was allowed through his seed of the adulterous marriage to make provisions as God raised up Solomon and permitted him to build the temple.

Can you identify in your life where God has taken a destruction of Satan and made it work for the good and the building up of your faith and trust in his ability to deliver us from our sins and continue victoriously just as his word promises.

"And the gates of hell shall not prevail against the church of God", and people think it's safe not to acknowledge God and reverence him in worship in his tabernacle, which is each of us, and in the affairs of our lives.

26. Patience Is A Virtue...Once Anything is Done, It Can't Be Undone... By Man

Count the cost before you make a choice because consequences always follow decisions whether good or bad, right or wrong. The testing of our faith builds patience as God unfolds his plans for us, we can't change yesterday's choices, we can only live each day one at a time and can't determine the future but only impact it as we choose wisely or foolishly. The attributes of time are in God's control alone and when we move ahead of his timing, we have complicated our life, not his purpose. God rewards us for obedience and faithfulness to him and when we are anxious even for those thing s that are needed, we tend to leave him out and pursue what we feel we deserve. We know that it is good for men and women to marry, but society reflects a 50 to 55% failure rate and many people are resolving the institution doesn't work. The problem isn't marriage; it's our refusing to place God at the head of our choices in marriage that relegate us to disappointment and disillusionment because we are not honoring his instructions for life. Marriage is a vow before God and man...next time you go to a wedding, listen to the words that join two people together...if they are from the bible. Many couples today want to say their own words, caught up in doing a good thing, the wrong way. God created marriage and said it is for a lifetime between one man and one woman, for richer or poorer, in sickness and in health, till death do us part, forsaking all others. It provides safety, sharing, learning, pleasure, commitment, trust, both emotionally and sexually, and productive successful rewards for the efforts of two people working and sacrificing together for a purpose and a plan. You can never get a STD from a faithful partner and some would dare to sleep around and insult a beautiful experience of trust, God calls it defilement of the marriage bed. If a man won't marry a woman before he sleeps with her, he is a fraud, and loves his own needs, more than the needs of the women his lying mouth says he loves. It is better not to make a vow, than to make a vow and not keep it...therefore, if you know you can't be faithful, don't marry and don't defraud anyone by pretense of love in sexual intimacy...God says sex is reserved for marriage, it is his gift to his creation and purpose, not for passions outside of its boundary. Can a woman once having been with a man return to her pure innocence before the act...only in a changed mind and heart that turns from a lifestyle of sin, and obediently trusting God's word as a lamp of light to her path of life, an act of forgiveness, only he can give to a new beginning. The bible teaches us that we will reap whatsoever we sow and to understand what the bible teaches will take much study and prayer that we might overcome the deep feelings of guilt and shame that imperfect lives have left us to manage...but that's why Jesus promised "I will never leave you or forsake you." How many friends, lovers or even family members have given this assurance and found it to be virtually impossible to keep?

Our world is full of many illusions and deception, even in the church, evil disguises itself as an angel of light, and it's only through patience that we can begin to discern the intentions and motives of people. We all have hidden behind facades, putting our best efforts forward, but the condition of man will not allow him to disguise his intentions indefinitely, we must listen closely to the things that are being said and demonstrated by the actions of those within our sphere of impact and influence. Out of the heart, the mouth speaks and out of the heart flow the issues of life.

The adventure of life is this...God gives us free choice, as long as we obey his commandments we prosper and stay under his protection in waiting patiently for his answers to our prayers, hopes, and dreams. He tells us that with every temptation..., which are of evil design, that he will provide a way of escape, so you must conclude this...if I know the right thing to do, yet I choose to do the wrong thing, then the root problem is the desire in my heart is evil. We hate to see ourselves as evil creatures, declaring how good we are and attempting to earn favor through good acts of kindness, but without the spirit of love, which is selfless, we are limited to be only selfish in our purpose. God tests us, not for his knowledge, but so that we can see ourselves. We move through life with frustrations and anxieties because we are distracted from the teachings of truth he tells us to follow, by the moment, daily, in all things we do. They are written in his word, but if we don't read it and believe and follow its instructions, how will we ever find happiness and joy in this life. There is a scripture in Isaiah that says righteousness and peace have kissed each other, realizing you can't have one without the other. To have patience with people and peace to enjoy this life, we must have right relationship with God and man, as much as is possible.

Psalms
37:4 Delight thyself also in the Lord, and he shall give thee the desires of thine heart.
37:5 Commit thy way unto the Lord trust also in him, and he shall bring it to pass.
37:7 Rest in the Lord, and wait patiently for him: fret not thyself because of him who prepareth in His way, because of the man who bringeth wicked devices to pass.

Philippians
4:8 Finally, brethren, whatsoever things are lovely, whatsoever things are of good report; if there be any virtue, and if there be any praise, think on these things.
4:9 those things, which ye have both learned, and received, and heard, and seen in me, do; and the God of peace shall be with you.

27. Still In Bondage To Sin

Did you know that we are in bondage to whatever lifestyle we choose to follow when we have disobeyed God's commandments and fail to exist and develop in his purpose for us? Slavery comes in many forms and fashions and because God allows us choice, we think we can do what we please or whatever we desire and in the end everything will be ok. This is not true however, and although we are not physically imprisoned, our minds are captive to negative patterns that take away the wonderful experiences of blessings we were designed to enjoy, without anticipating negative consequences. Because we have learned to choose to be happy, which is taking control of your emotions by refusing to be discouraged or running to escape the deep inner thoughts that speak to us of needed changes in our circumstances...better defined as denial or even pride, which people do in the party lifestyle, we ignore our conscience and continue down a slow subtle path of eventual destruction and defeated lives. You wake up one morning to look in the mirror of reality and see how time has broken down the facade that hid the internal pain of failed relationships and wasted years. How long will this season of insecurity and hidden truth last? We overlook a greater achievement of joyfulness in this life that God promises when we delight in him and turn away from selfish ambitions that are fed at the expense of others we have defrauded. We make excuses for bad conduct sexually such as, its just my nature, I was lonely, I deserve it, it felt so good I couldn't stop, I needed someone to help me forget the last relationship, or the worst one, everybody is doing it, and think we have justified our actions, but the inner person is slowly being lost to hardened emotions that scar internally and hide themselves in greed and self pity.

An innocent mind towards God is too precious to carelessly allow the influences of this polluted world to steal, but so frequently that is just what happens to most people as they mature and reflect on the past mistakes that have left broken hearts and dreams. Wrong is wrong, even if everyone is doing it, right is right, even if nobody is doing it. God is whom we will answer to, not man, and who can know if the future will bring another opportunity for change. It is fact that for people who never have a spiritual experience prior to becoming young adults, that rarely later in life do they become Christians, and set beliefs are ingrained even if erroneous in concept. Did you know the bible tells of God giving unbelievers over to idolatry to whatever their understanding has put faith in? Is it another person, money, lifestyle, religion, even self that possess your confidence? Let them rescue you from calamity or disaster when it has overtaken you. God is real, and he is a jealous God and in his judgment against those who deny him, which is always fair, he warns of giving hardened hearts over to a reprobate mind, in which the condition of a person's attitude is fixed on his own destruction. His mercy is amazing that even allowing a person to destroy fleshly desires, his purpose ultimately is to save the soul in the end. Why would anyone risk such a painful correction and waste his purpose to glorify God in this life?

I have heard the stories of many young couples that find that long searched for love with someone, only to discover the past involvement with others has left guilt and shame that prevents the total enjoyment of intimacy in the most important relationship we can experience in this natural life. Intimacy is emotional, spiritual, intellectual, and physical as well, and when any of these characteristics are damaged or missing in marriage, we struggle to enjoy what God intended as a blessing and reward for obedience to his design for marriage, love, and sex. Why wait? Did you know that in the Garden of Eden, which was paradise, the perfect existence of man and woman in harmony with each other, nature, and God, but sex was never even discovered as they enjoyed utopia we have all strived to attain in pursuit of intimate relationship and pleasure? Can you visualize a man and a woman, naked together, unashamed, and God allowing them to learn about each other on a purposeful mission of togetherness with order and design to build and populate a world, and giving sex a proper time to be explored? Read the story and you will see that after God had driven them from Paradise, then Adam knew Eve, and she conceived.

It takes two people to raise a child, and anyone foolish to think they can do it alone, easily, has already overloaded their plate for the critical years a child needs to prepare for the future. It's hard enough as a couple, but to ignore God and deny the child a hope for tomorrow is a responsibility no-one else can strategically or effectively provide, and we allow this evil world to capture our most precious blessing that God has given us to be faithful stewards over, to train and instruct. So busy with drama and your babies are watching everything, because they know when you're not with them, you're making somebody or something else a priority and they begin to question what they are worth and what is important becomes distorted. Can you see the evolvement of negative generational cycles that leave gaps in the development of whole empowered individuals?

There are so many things I have experienced in my own life, and I am still determined to build people up, not tear them down, but sometimes it becomes difficult to stay focused when I have connected with someone in a way such as I know I have with you, especially when I am aware of the spiritual battles we fight and the seductive nature of evil we can't defeat standing alone. The bible tells us not to defraud one another, but most people don't live by the book, so deception is all around us, and the good we would do is hindered by natural desires that are not under the discipline of God. "There is a way that seems right to a man, but the end thereof is death." We first die spiritually because of sin, but for those who trust God, eternal life is promised at the end of this life. It teaches us that in Christ, "we are a new creation, old things are past away, behold, all things are new. Why wouldn't everyone want a chance to have a new start and hope? It teaches us that Satan has "blinded the world with deception", and people can't see the condition we are in.in actuality...the blind are leading the blind, and together they are walking towards the edge of danger and eternal separation from God.

Chp. 4   Waters of Consciousness

28. Bliss

A man once said, "I haven't done a thing in life that I wanted to do." I had to ask myself this question pertaining to that statement, why would one not live life comfortable with their actions, decisions, and being? People everyday work their jobs, doing for 40 hours a week or more, to retire at 60 years of age if lucky. The 40 to 60 plan is as common as scrambled eggs and bacon, 365 days a year not including sick leave, paid days off and vacation time. Why is this I ask? Do we obtain certification after certification, and degree after degree, all to promote and sale ourselves via a resume', in order to serve under someone else's coat. As products of society we tend to follow every social and economical trend in order to maintain ourselves within the stride of society. Why do we follow in synchronization like the ant to the rule of today or the task of tomorrow? We are locked into a time and space continuum coming and going, leaving and doing 95% of the time for someone or something else. When is it, that we find time for ourselves in todays fast past society? Just an hour of the day to yourself in your very own special place, away from income issues, phone calls, televisions, and or everyday problems we face, would relieve not only stress from your life but add a few years to it as well. People often say, "A lazy man can not gain anything in life" which is actually a biblical quote but in today's blue and white-collar work environments the feeling of security is always on edge. Based not on ones productivity or giving you're full out effort to a business or corporation but more times than none it comes down to that old saying, "It's not what you know but whom you know." So the question that remains in us all is, when do I find my place of bliss? I'm not speaking of nirvana nor heaven no, this place exist right here on earth within us all, we just forgot how to find its place of residence, due to our complex and structured lives. Living every waking moment programmed and displayed on a screen of economics, consumerism, corporation brain washings, societal pressures to conform to it's politically correctness amongst other things, and a race for time that seems to speed up as our lives become more and more complex. The problem we face is that, we've placed so many things into our baskets that we forgot about time in its relationship to energy. We have become so task driven that are very life's energy, has been reduced to somewhat of a dormant state, not allowing it to function and rejuvenate naturally and correctly. You can not imagine what we are doing to ourselves in this continual way of living day to day, rushing, microwaving, fast fooding, quick cashing, needing everything now, instantly and directly leading an assault on our own mind and body. Is this just a process of evolution towards the function of this society? Have we forgotten about bliss, peace, and what true beauty is? Or have we replaced the smells, the sights, and the sounds with virtual simulations created by our own mental CGI (computer generated intelligence.) Are those who live in third world countries, rain forest and or those who dwell earth's rich and vast plains simply rebels against time? Or do they know something we have lost in our pursuit of wealth, global expansion, multibillion dollar high rises, shinier faster vehicles, data and information at the speed light, sex and fantasy on an Internet island. Everything literally at the tip of man's finger, so why would we need to slow down? Isn't arrogance the confidence we need for success in a self made dog eat dog and cat world? Who needs a God now?

29. Blame us all

To often
Do we as people
Take life
For granted
Take time for granted
Not grasping to
That
Precious moment
That
Important minute
That
Which now is lost
Why?

The environment one and some
Are intertwined into
Can be devastating
Without knowing
Without an effort of consciousness
A mere lack of understanding
The braking point
Of failed action, love, patience, and belief
Failure to seek, to find, to follow
And Fear
GOD

How quickly does the split second
Of time take form
Take life
Take forever it seems
To correct
Who's to blame?
Society
Yes
Poverty
Yes
The lack of Opportunity
Yes
We

Us

Yes

-Dedicated to two lives lost, little precious lives all but three months old, now in GOD's hands

Akira and **Alexia Noel.** Twin babies found dead at home off of Franklin Blvd. in their crib, due to neglect and a lack of assistance from the city, state, and we the people, we the community.

-Errol V. Moore Jr.

30. Flee From Youthful Passion

Yesterday is gone...just like a bird, spreading it's wings to soar into the heavens...upward...out of sight. It is reduced to memories of information, accessible only in reflections for today...to move us into the future more productively... history...still, the time we spend is no longer available...like money spent.

Eternity awaits somewhere.

They say that when we die, without knowing the truth, we open our eyes again only to the great white throne of judgment...

How long have you been asleep...only, a moment in time, a twinkle of the eye...in forevermore...

Conclusion...If you saw the play...you want to miss the real event.

Transition of mind and body, who has the last say? Your mind or your head...

You know what I'm sayin'...not wanting these thoughts...what it felt like to be Black.

Never letting you forget being too Black or not Black enough

No hang'n out...no get'n high...no rhythm...no parties...

Can't do nothing except go to school...do chores...and oh...

Sleep'n in church, dreaming about what I'm miss'n...

Couldn't even appreciate the godfather of soul...

Now...that's to Black for some...gyration, slide'n, sweat'n, doing the splits...scream'n..."I feel good"...

Early reflection of a gifted and diverse culture searching for it's value, and purpose...out of slavery...sharecropping...transition through oppression. Need'n a national direction...a position of ...validation...yeah...some make it through the cracks successfully, but what was that hair all about?

A pompadour, a chute, the process, an Afro, a natural...regression to the jerry-curl...

Thank God MJ made bald fashionable.

I recall a whole lot of us brothers got lost in identity crisis...

Wasn't no choice of gender question...a man is a man...

Cry'n out in ways "subliminally" indoctrinated before the term was popular...

Searching for acceptance or just fitting into a fad...compromised,

Some of you young brothers can't even remember Uncle Tom, but every one wearing the label was someone's relative. Those names hurt."Nigger," only sounds good... with militant.

Some cultures today use'n labels our folk died for... to snatch the word out your mouth, cause they won't be no white man's nigger no mo.so you and me don't have to...

Validate...belong to...comradery...partners and homies...

I am a nation...a culture...an entity...an individual...not an enigma of choice or appropriation.

Get your foot off my neck, land of the free...free to profile...you feel me?

Every aspect of a people is relative...

Ignorance... killed Dr. King, he presented us with a "Dream"...

Educate and love me father...love and nurture me mother with your gentle sensitivity, empower my future with wisdom you have gained, so that my resource unified is a pool of richness that can save and build a nation, a history a legacy of prosperity and success. All American cultures cooperating together "One nation, under God, indivisible, with liberty and justice for all."

Why a Rev. Dr. Martin Luther King?

God looks into the future...like only he can, and he saw today, the unbalanced focus on liberty for all, but the justice has been spiritually abandoned, and liberty of individuals perversions is impacting all morals.

He presented to us a hope of unity, solidarity, and pride to a progressive move of non-violent revolt...

Would we even remember if they hadn't made his memory a holiday?

"Dare to dream Black people," loose those mental chains that destroy homes and incarcerate a young force at a higher cost than it would take to educate them...it took his murder to help lift that foot...

But our taste for the precious life of selfish indulgence and comfort has compromised our focus, value, and morals.

Can you see me? I am not a stud...not a myth...I don't want to sex you up...I want to lift you up.

They couldn't see James, some thought he was a joke...an invisible man, but the song says...

"I knew that I would"... confidence, he had a gift, a song and a dance... and lived a dream.

You better get a song...might even learn to dance...cause life, isn't a joke...

The word tells us to sing melody to God through this troubled life...

If we don't change...a whole lot of tears are ahead, and to much pleasure spoils...and everyone eventually gets to old to be the "hardest working man in show business."

Caged in paternal belief traditions, foolishly wondering if there is a God...

Emulating and perpetuating high profile role models, avant-garde...

Good, bad, or ugly...everybody can't be like Mike...one percent of the world includes pro athletes, rap artists, and movie stars...you got to have a dream...but while following after high hopes, you got to have a job to survive, to increase...don't despise small beginnings, an infant is helpless at birth.

So you better get an education or all the information you can absorb... so you can deal...

What we need is for men and women to be in house to teach their children, instead of perpetuating immature patterns late into their 40's... children questioning what is right, what is truth, and no parent available, forcing them to make adult choices with insufficient information on what "love" is all about.

Lakisha had a baby at 13 girl..."who's her baby's daddy?" She don't know... one of those boys on the corner...

Doomed to poverty, without support, without changing your belief... looking for love, wanting to be wanted.

No daddy there to say "baby don't give up," life gives hard lessons, but you can make it...you're special to me, I will help you through this, I love you daughter.

Did you know you don't have to teach a child how to do wrong...we are born with a sin nature...

You just have to leave him alone, no instruction, no truth, no values, and no purpose...

You don't have to murder a man to kill him...just take away his hope... just don't do anything.

Like a Lyndon B. Johnson...recognize a people's problem Daniel Patrick Moynihan...

And a free nation establishes a policy of "benign neglect"...

Problems don't work themselves out.

Genocide is a slow process, oppression creates resilience to ignorance

A great people refuse to die...education is equal information...not level opportunity. Selma...Montgomery...Newark...Memphis...Rio Linda...Elk Grove!

Can you trust a man with the same skin, the same blood?

Ask Abel, the first murder...

Remember Marvin, JFK, Bobby, Martin, Little Conner or Lacy!

Unresolved problems...kill people.

Blonde hair, blue eyes fantasy...society dictating to the impressionable mind " it's" idea of beauty...

"I'm ugly"...big lips, wide nosed, dark skin, hair like wool...over developed gluteus,

I'm polluted, diluted, permeated with images that are unattainable... my windows confuse perception, and the subliminal is in control...is my identity my dark skin, my sexuality, my hatred in ignorance of my culture, my choices that hide reality or is it...

Who I am?

In my nation inclusive of my ethnicity I am an entity as unique as a single star in millions of galaxies...but do I know this? Certain men mock creation, attempting to impose upon us sick interpretations of identity...

Burning in their lustful passion of choice...

Nature knows purpose is lost without productivity, "good fruit"...

It's a principle unchangeable as gravity, by God's laws...even if all mankind participates...

A dog in heat will attempt to mount anything, yet you never seen the same gender submit, they step away and look almost to say, "dog what is your problem...can't you see I'm a dog made just like you"

All animals' work with is instinctive nature...still they're intelligent enough not to defy nature.

Man child metamorphosis...passion, desire out of control, consuming my purpose...

Wet dreams so real...so sweet... you wonder how a boy discovers himself one night, experiencing ecstasy in his loins... no wonder a man will often want to roll over and fall asleep after making love to his wife... childhood reflections...selfish apex of the body...lower level of awareness of true intimacy...

Somebody should have told me...but sex has been stolen from the beauty of marriage and shameful images steal delightful memories of discovering her...as she discovers me.

But why is pornography so popular?   Reality requires more involvement, and a real woman wants pleasures when with her man, but a selfish male...think only of himself.

1969...Black is beautiful...college women, sisters, fine, intelligent, educated, curious, open-minded, available...revelation...Focus lost... breezys' everywhere...unbridled lust my mission.

Who am I? What am I? No looking over my shoulder for my preacher father...any rules...

Girl I just want to...girl...did you know it was" that thing"...

Not you...could have been any female that looked good for that moment...

Dog in heat...driven by a nature that couldn't even...be understood..."somebody should have told me."

Fella's mackin' hoes...playin' everything...everything real... your folks, each other, ultimately yourself.

Conscience speaks to me in mama's voice, "boy you know those fellas don't know the Lord, don't fool around with any girl you don't want to marry"...

I was mama's baby boy and I always knew she loved me, so I

Listened, but I didn't understand...so I married the one it was easiest to get to...cause she made me feel so good, it had to be love...she gave me all her time and I never felt like this before...baby does anything I want... and the freak in me, matches the freak in her...watch out if she can't say I love you, if she don't say I love you...unexpressed silence speaks loud, and passionate whispers of desire can address anger towards another, that youth often can not understand, and trying to do a right thing the wrong way, misses the mark spiritually...not considering the consequences deceitfully waiting to escape, like opening Pandora's box...

And sex is not physical alone, but spiritually it joins mind, soul, and body, and outside of marriage, it becomes a curse, and the fruit born to a cursed relationship is deprived of the beauty of creation and over complicates opportunity designed for family unity...Somebody should have told me.

I listen to your words of passion, young love thinks it can swim oceans and once leaving the safety of the beach with anxious energy and hope, soon discovers heavy strokes in the deep waters, no land in sight, and floating on your back only produces drifting in a squall... unbalanced drive can stir your life in directions you can not see in the present...Yea, I thought I could handle my challenges of relationship and building new love, the red flags we ignore for passions of sex...but those flaws of character can not be satisfied...they consume their victim until obsessed it becomes their strongest motivation...like a drug...the addiction...just one more time...just one more...just one..."Oh God"...just give it to me, I don't care...anybody, I need it...where is it?

"It can not be satisfied." In this imperfect world we attempt to nurture and fix others on our mission of potentials and ideal experience, investing precious time in labor of hope that one day soon a light will come on in the life of someone we desire...but if a light isn't shining when you find them...you better move on, cause the only changes that you can control and adjust to are your own.

Eloquent words of expressions of deep intimacy revealing the secret emotions of intellectually, articulate, well educated, deep thinkers, with idiosyncratic thoughts and reflections of idealistic visions of encounters of a man and his way with a woman...but don't you see...sex without commitment allows an escape route for insecure people relegated to selfish pleasures at the expense of some victim who dared to care and attempt to love, with risk and reckless abandon for their own well being, emotions, health, values, morals, trust, confidence, self-esteem, sexuality, and sanity...at the expense of losing dignity, identity, a priceless name, and a promising future with someone else who could truly care and love them...your treasured feelings, flapping in the winds of life issues like a flag on a pole in a storm, reducing dreams to shattered hope, shame, despair, worthlessness, and guilt, knowing you should have made a wiser choice...but you didn't... and we don't...where does it end...can it really get that bad?

Are you willing to risk it?

Interacting in relationship with toxic people so crazy and thoughtlessly selfish, they make you believe...you're crazy.

Years have passed I don't even care to remember, heartbreak I thought would never end...rebounding...tail tucked between my legs...Black queen or Black widow...

Damaged confidence, produces devastated children with damaged confidence, and foothills become mountains in our paths.

Black family...are we stumbling forward blindly or falling backwards... deeper into despair...

Can't you see our pain? Can your laughter hide the truth and your facade conceals reality within?

For some...this poem is your future, it is what tomorrow will bring... because most of you won't hear me, thinking, that's so sad...until somebody tosses a rock in your glass house.

I work so hard to hold on...just like Alicia Keyes says..."people think success suddenly happens cause they don't see the hard work before the recognition."

Time is just like holding water in your hands...hard to get a good drink before it's gone. Can't you hear Mother Nature's disappointment... the grand old lady is dying and I isn't seen no graceful grandmas...

Still getting their freak on, except on Jerry Springer...and it isn't pretty. Women's liberation or nervous breakdown...always saying it's hard to find a good man...if I could just get a good man...

Would you know one if you saw one? It takes time for those coverings to drop, for the real character to reveal itself clearly, then once damaged by the whirlwind romance everything after it is..."too good to be true." Biggest misconception of the independent woman striking out to conquer male dominance by asserting her liberal freedom is...a man needs to find you. Preparation is being ready to make him appreciate you and earn your devotion through his commitment to you, because anything to easily acquired, will not be valued..."proving you love him with sex never works, having his baby won't keep him at home, and testing the waters before marriage almost assures complicating intimacy if he ever actually buys the ring.

Women must protect their self-value as a treasure or they will lose the precious spirit of freedom to love, joy to develop, and hope to share dreams.

Some 25 years or more of liberation, and most of what I've seen is overcorrecting...women were right in that struggle for recognition...but what's Mocha women of color all about. Some wise women trying to get back to the family...the time hasn't changed men, 200 years couldn't... and the Black family is worst off now more than ever. My Black queen left to find what she had missed at 30...and the mission still proceeds almost 20 years later, and the 3rd generation is experiencing the fallout of broken family. I've heard it all...somebody bigger, younger, a new beginning...funny thing them single girlfriends who encouraged her to party...cause I was a hard working square...some of them married now, with children, and have slowed way down. My ex, still trying to hang last I heard. Yeah, I've seen a lot...tall dark and handsome...really meant anybody taller than me, because I represented a paternal authority in my ex-wife's comprehension and her accountability to me was skewed and expressed in words like..."you're not my father." I never tried to be...she just wanted her "independence." Well...I'm just a square that God had pity for, after straying so far from the path my dilemma overwhelmed my strength, and I reached the end of myself. His hands everywhere I go, in people placed in my path to help lift a broken sinner off his knees to give him hope...and a new dream.

My young brothers and sisters...do you think the ability to articulate specific aspirations and stimulation of awareness of the dynamics of a man and a woman will produce a vehicle to realize upward mobility in a sensual society in pursuit of reciprocal selfish ambitious pleasures to attain the idealistic goals accomplishing utopian fantasies and euphoric experiences within your personal sphere of influence that have eluded man's quest from the beginning of time until today, discounting his inevitable motive of greed, power, and idolatry to rule and dominate over the unfortunate and vulnerable victims of deceptions of the heart and emotional struggles, revealing itself in the ultimate manifestation of our obsession with self, driving us to our destruction? Why would any woman want to take on the frustrations and enigma's of a confrontational male gender experience of existence...didn't a woman...Eve, eat the forbidden fruit first...woman's first desire for wisdom and self accomplished attaining of knowledge..."the need to know."

The subtle mystery of God's appointment for man is not hidden, but discovered in obedience...not trusting the Creator's plan...results in consequences we can not understand or escape.

Today's woman knows something Eve did not know...there is no longer an excuse...knowledge is available everywhere, and choices are within the individuals control of paths to pursue...the Devil didn't make you do it, and he is not omnipresent as some would believe. Man is still attempting to return to the garden that God drove us from...but refuses to realize only God can bring Paradise to fruition...

Do you refuse to see the truth? Do you refuse to see me?

I am a Godly man, with character, gifts, and full of love for others...my heart is no longer torn between my heads...my desire is under discipline...I am waiting patiently for you to see...

So that I can love you...God's way...for man's way is impossible to know.

This life system thinks we don't need Jesus...

And this world believes we don't need a savior.

E.V.M.

31. Good-bye Mom...See You in Heaven

I saw an angel pass.
I couldn't see her wings, yet...
I felt the wind as she breezed through.
A transformation...
A passing over...
From life, into life eternal...
As God's breath...
Returned unto Him.

He sent it out...
Only for a season...
A time to accomplish...
His purpose.

As I sought to grasp the vision...
That I could not understand...
I could not see her wings,
But...I saw her face...
Shining bright with glory...
Not death...
But life.

Into his presence return...
His gift of time...
His power over all life.

The Rabbi on a ship tossed to and fro in the tempest...
The men aboard run to him in fear, to find him asleep...
"Lord, care thou not we perish?"
He stretches his arms as he rises...he yawns...he speaks a command,
a soft word to calm the storm...

"Peace be still"...and the wind and sea obey.
Turning to the men he questions their doubt...
"Didn't I say we were going to... the other side?"

God has not promised skies blue,
 Flower stewn pathways all our lives through.

86

But, God has promised...
Rest, for the weary, strength for the weak...
Undying sympathy, undying love.
Do not stand at my grave and weep...
I am not there...
I do not sleep...
I am the wind blowing over the hill...
I am the bird rustling in the bush...
I am the stars up in the sky.

-Errol Moore Sr.

32. Independent Compromised Nation of Individuals

It is historical fact that every great civilization is eminently destroyed from within. Great military states have proven to be included within this record as victim of moral decay, as whole societies fell to the demand of liberal moral agendas, demanding its individual rights, at the expense of traditional established national values and mores. In fact, the truths of creation and purpose of man to dwell together in unity and mutual prosperity are lost in distortions of intellectual beliefs that satisfy lusts of selfish, ambitious, permissive platforms, attempting to swallow up anything in its path that opposes its acceptance. In a game of reverse psychology the focus is now on forcing liberal values on society, rather than maintaining constitutional creeds our nation was founded, developed, and built to greatness on. We find ourselves today in the U.S., facing the same crisis as these predecessor cultures and civilizations, tracking a pattern we are ignoring as metaphorically, a "giant sleeps." So goes the family, so goes the nation.

Marriage is an institution of success by design and purpose, and from its inception in the Garden it provides man and woman with the only true opportunity to join together in paradise, and harmony to prosper individuals through commitment to vows and boundaries established by a perfect creator. He gave this gift to us in perfect order, just as everything he has ever created is good, but our sinful human nature and qualities fail to acknowledge His divine presence within this bond of accountability and responsibility to Him as authority. Our failures as individuals to submit to each other in love and respect derails a beautiful opportunity for building productive homes and lives we can enjoy in this lifetime. Seek ye first, the kingdom of Heaven and His righteousness and all these things will be added unto you. Just as Eve's selfish ambition for wisdom failed to trust God's warnings, our failure to obedience to the bible, jeopardizes and ruins our dreams of love, romance, and prosperity. It is in fact," unwedded," that is a failure, and alternatives to traditional and biblical standards that are ruining our society.

In the 1960's as women's rights began to mount its platform for independence, equality, and a voice, the agendas joining the struggle by jumping on board in combining supports, have risen to positions of power and influence, such as the ACLU, Gay Rights, and Equal Rights, and the free sex explosion has become a cesspool of VD, unfaithfulness, and abortions. Some positive results have improved conditions within society, while more critical conditions have been neglected and impacted by escalating warnings of destructive patterns. The family, "the country," is in shambles of turmoil while these groups continue to pursue their agendas aggressively pushing the needs of coming generations aside for zealous desires of moral freedoms that defy mans procreation. Women in the late 60's were just looking for fairness and equality in the home, from tyrannical men and customs that truly were unbiblical, as ignorance of leadership attributes were propagated, and 4 decades later the independently driven woman has abandoned her children to day cares, and often men who attempt to plug an impossible role to fill without instinctive attributes. In the 70's, demands escalated to independence, freedom from traditional roles and values, and equality in the workplace. In the 80's, self control was gone and now you can hear, "I want my own," leaving husbands and children for careers to pursue independent quests of economic upward mobility, a false solution to fulfillment, and today you can witness lifestyles manifested by these choices have led to sexual greed and distortion of traditional moral roles by women. Over correction means two wrongs cannot make a right. Women are acting as though they are men in aggressive pursuit of other women and morally doing what men did for decades outside of the family within the so called freedom of individual rights. Double standards have always existed, and the so-called freedom has ruined families and individual self-worth, despite society efforts to mask the guilt and shame with tolerance and permissiveness. Doesn't the bible tell us that a good name is better than riches? The fun and youth of life doesn't last forever, but society makes us wear labels for a lifetime. A man can and still will act like a "dog," sleeping around with any number of women he can, and society refers to him as an escort, gigolo, ladies man, and player, considers him successful and accepted by his peers as an example to follow, and most women will still give him an opportunity to build a relationship, while the same behavior by a women will produce devastating consequences and leaves her labeled a whore, a prostitute, and a freak, and she is shunned by society as valueless and most men won't want to consider her for marriage.

The gay lifestyle in the 60's was so concealed to the common public as not to even pose a threat, the defined terminology, "in the closet", hidden behaviors unacceptable in mainstream society. In the 70's, jumping on the women's movement and somehow attempting to associate choice with identity, the equal rights bandwagon. Today they are asking for equal rights in marriage opportunities that will destroy the core of natural reproduction and the institution that perpetuates the cycles of man's existence. They demand tolerance for their activities at the expense of values that promote healthy development of our children, pushing to teach so called, "alternative lifestyles," in our schools, to the innocent, immature, undeveloped, attempting to push legislation that redefines abuse to impose sexual values that are indoctrinated on victims of societies reckless neglect. The media has become an open airway for their platform and the permissive openness is exposing and polluting young minds with propaganda of an "affectionate placement," to the emotionally weak, and sick, that they can influence with hope of acceptance through a sexual choice, because of complicated issues of male, female, dynamics that are normal challenges of cultural construction.

A key factor in the demise of structure or " cultural construction," not commonly exposed by media circles is the moral position of the woman. One of the last defenses against moral chaos or anarchy is the female role and position defined within societies traditional standards. Women are not designed to lead families as providers and protectors in vital developmental years of offspring's, not minimizing her gifts or skills to maintain careers professionally, and exceptionally, at the proper timing. Their critical role in the home is to keep it functioning successfully, and to equip the home with an atmosphere of pleasantness, harmony, organization, and family unity, with diversified social skills essential for offspring empowerment to flourish in future endeavors with confident readiness as they launch out into life's arenas. The dual role of provider and maintaining family balance too often overloads the effectiveness of the designed nurturer and placed in an environment with jungle like survival instincts, many emotionally vulnerable women can lose focus of purpose. The jungle can eat the gullible woman alive with deep issues of guilt in recognizing ineffective order or overwhelming pressures, and escape is often sought as solution to demands of sacrificial, delayed gratification as the idealistic perfection is drowned in reality of unending responsibilities, scheduling, and organization. Many young women, often neglected or ill prepared in personal development become so lost and disillusioned with the dreams they nurtured from early youth, of marriage, love, children, economics, and romance, that they abandon ship in an ocean of turbulence, feeling they have failed, not realizing the impossible mission of complete control, but building and developing systematic processes is overlooked, just to stand on anything that offers support or relief from workloads of responsibility at home. The family today is failing; tomorrow it will be the nation. Men have been irresponsible in leadership, and authority, producing children, and leaving the responsibility to women forced to maintain households inadequately provided for, economically, spiritually, and socially, and the X generation is the byproduct of divorce and failed development of our homes, local neighborhood schools, churches, and government. A recent interview with a nationally known expert on sociological patterns and trends of society concluded that the current wave of depraved actions and thinking are restricted only to traditional beliefs and values taught within the family structure. As these boundaries fall to public exposures of liberal degradation, a diluted result will occur within society. Ignorance is not based on intellect, but on the lack of information. We must research the development and direction our nation is headed and be actively involved in political and religious arenas where we can influence decisions that impact our lives subjectively to objectively reorder purpose, structure, and stability.

Ultimately, the escalating spread of child pornography, and sexually explicit literature, reflects man's inability to stay within established boundaries, resulting in depraved behavior spreading. Our children are being solicited by the liberal cry for moral freedom's selfish indulgence, defining sexually explicit exposure as harmless entertainment. Any illness that goes untreated runs the inevitable risk of escalating into dangerous life threatening health issues when the body's natural immune defenses are ineffective in fighting the invasion. Pornography is a wide spreading virus striking down everyone in its path, an illness that is not being treated on a national scale because its dollar value speaks as an industry, ignoring its destructive decay. " Freedom of choice"..."freedom of choice," rings out as millions of lives are cut down by abortion, and go ignored, for the convenience of irresponsible decisions, defiantly raging our children and grandchildren should be allowed to decide for themselves by giving them information on behavioral patterns that are unscriptural in origin, as the ACLU does everything within it's power to remove anything biblical from public institutions and national foundational articles and processes. Already, in Canada, laws against religious convictions and beliefs are punishing the rights of individuals who refuse service to anyone with opposing positions of traditional values, to the extent of teaching or preaching against popularly accepted behaviors of untraditional lifestyles, and is being legislatively prohibited. When will these laws cross our borders and infiltrate judicial legislation to permit any and every choice of freedom to do anything that pleases the illness of alternative lifestyle choices?

We as parents can't sit back and allow coming generations to inherit permissive liberality that destroys the institution of family, as we know it. We are responsible. We must make a stand that says, "I want to inform and teach my children the right values for life and will not allow men with immoral agendas to establish their future learning fields." Children can not make a mature choice." Based on knowledge of life that is inexperienced, we are their guide, council, and safety. They are developing to be prepared for their adult years, requiring us to be their hope for truth and information.

E.V.M.

　　If you were taking a long trip without a map and all you could rely on is your recall from a previous experience, would you allow your child to make the decision which direction to take? Isn't life this same journey? We never hate people, we hate the wrong things they stand for and that they choose to do, as they strive to compromise our values, by permitting and excepting errant erratic values of current platform issues.

33. Man's Shortsighted Understanding of The Bible...and His Own Glory

Recently returning from a family reunion in Birmingham, Al., we found ourselves held over in New Orleans waiting on a plane delayed in Florida by bad weather. As I observed my young nephew, who had brought along his 11 month old son to the reunion, and his attentiveness, care and patience, administered to the helpless toddler, I began reflecting upon the experience and the many levels of relating to the family members I know so little about. Our parents have in most part all past on, and we are now, with the few remaining, the leaders and examples of wise counsel that God has builder up to take the family into the future. The dilemma present is this; the family is struggling to survive. Not many strong male examples are present and the women are frustrated with, for the most part, holding things together emotionally, economically, and spiritually. The younger men and women are opinionated and self accomplishes as a whole, and education and easily attained prosperity has left them dangerously lacking in spiritual matters and in understanding of life's consequences approaching them in their future. With so many in the family either victims of divorce in the preceding generation or struggling to resolve issues in a current over-complicated marriage or relationship, the younger group is willing to stand where they are to anticipate the future and see no real need to address the questions and thoughts they should be bringing to us about life. The mentors they are looking to are peers who have attained worldly knowledge and success, and the separation of generations is clearly what they desire, although they will acknowledge affectionately, a hierarchy.

Sharing my observations with my nephew resulted in an interesting position and response, hopefully leaving him challenged to look deeper into his bible for understanding his position as a believer. He was questioning his ability to accomplish the ministry God has placed in him and had not recognized his weaknesses were God's strengths in building his walk through many trials and adversities to the development of leadership design critical in this life. He had concluded the younger people as a whole are set in their beliefs and could not see the walls that must be torn down, one at a time, being constructed in false security, and the mission we are all called to pursue and serve in God's plan. He presented to me a scenario that had taken place on his job in reaction to his stand for the truth. An older person he had obviously shared his faith with, in an animated attempt to discredit the bible, had grabbed two books, one a dictionary, the other of course, the bible, and slapped them down next to each other on a counter, proclaiming the bible had no historical value, and raising the dictionary in one hand to triumphantly proclaim its relevance as more valuable. My young nephew was stumped in his response and perhaps even walked away without defending his faith, but does the bible need to be defended in such a shortsighted demonstration of comparison by someone God has not chosen, at least at that moment, to reveal the truth of his word. Typically, most people who dispute the bible have never actually even read the book they are doubting, and for those who have attempted, they fail to understand that comprehension is attained spiritually in God's time, with diligence and persistence in seeking truth by divine intervention, not logical interpretation of natural perception.

The only thoughts I could leave with my nephew to encourage his stand and support his position on the truth were the only thoughts I believe God gave me at the moment. "Can you open a dictionary with all its words and definitions from A to Z, and find an answer to any issue of life that never fails?" Will it organize with purpose itself or must someone comprehensively design its intent? No! It's not possible. The bible however is not just a historical record of generations of people just like success, their failures and us as they acknowledge God's direction for their lives. In reading about the beginnings of man and his choices we can discern how the bible is a map for life and purpose for mans creation even today, to lead and assist us to fruitful and productive existence within the family and society, that all might be given the opportunity to know the Creator of man, and the dictionary...I wonder if the man knew that God allowed Adam to name all the animals...interesting they are still called the same till this day.

34. Point Break

Tolerance, is it a fear or a reserve? Is it based off of emotion or a state of mind? Are some of us more patient than others when it comes to the acceptance of pain, suffering and extreme annoyance? When a child grabs hold of the tail, of a dog or a cat and the dog yelps but the cat turns around and immediately scratches the little child, was that a point of breaking for the feline animal? What about the dog? Is it fair enough to say that, the dog was either in fear of the child or was holding back its anger in reserve and understanding of its point break? I believe that this action or non-action is what we as human beings fight with everyday to an extent. For an animal to react in a violent or passive manor we normally remove question in great detail, or forget about the moment very easily. With the exception of a mauling or severe violent rage, which often finds some airtime on our local news channels. Since we have more understanding when it comes to action or non-action, we as humans are not given the same leeway in societies eye. Our reasoning coupled with a consciousness of our actions gives us ample time to determine our point of breaking. We are fully aware of our actions be it deranged or a blind rage. There are some people that have very complex mental disorders but, these individuals also have what we all have and that are a spirit and a consciousness. I myself can admit to having some serious thoughts of a deformed and violent pattern of action, based off of fear or an angered emotional state. Without having a level of reasoning these actions could have taken place. We all have had these same points in our lives, young and old alike, for we are human beings with complexities that more often than none are unexplainable in it's depths. This is the very reason why any kind of influence, drug related or the like, is very dangerous when we our confronted with our point of breaking. There are those who feel that a person that doesn't react to certain situations is either a cowardly person or harshly a "bitch". Little do the unwise know that, fear itself is a conscious level of reserve, that if unleashed could cause severe violence for either party involved. Could you for moment imagine the point of breaking for one who has been enslaved, after being witness to the brutal murder of his wife children or vise versa? Not unless you have actually experienced something so horrific can you gather the pain and anger that certainly was ready to burst like a firm ripe cherry tomato that is caught between the sole of a shoe and the ground beneath it. In this instance there is little escape from this type of pain and anger except, some quite time and space outside of those who are not in your best interest at the time. The very reason why we need discipline as human beings is so that, we may become wise enough to understand ourselves. This is where the prison system has lost itself. I don't care how you bake it, flip it, fry it, mash it or toast it, incarceration in not conducive at all to the proper forms of mental harmony. Could you gather yourself to the realization that life outside of your cell would continue its course without you? Now that's some harsh reality one would to face everyday, for a particular period of time or in some cases life without any chance of parole. Image that, now tell me, or better yet measure for me the magnitude of the point break when, your world is gone, life now has no meaning, nor do the melodies of a favorite sound sweet with the sun gleaming against your face as a cool wind breeze swiftly crosses over your entire face carrying with it the smell of freedoms aroma's.

35. The BIG IF?

What does time really permit? Are you aware that today can be gone tomorrow? Lost and wiped out without any notice or care, just like that! We have absolutely no control over what is the IF? Let me pose this question to you, "Are you prepared?" We are all searching for something, but what? We are all at the complete disposal of the uncontrollable, the IF? We have all been blessed, to have lived up until now with the same unknowns that has plagued and baffled

The human mind for centuries. Many hours of discussion through forums, debates and blogs with the primary intent centered around the dissection and analyzation of the unanswerable. To the point of exhaustion with much failure towards any conclusion about these unknowns, the IF. The only certain IF, we are sure of is that of death which will eventually come knocking for us all. The second

Known fact of course is that you were born, and do to the fact that you are reading this book and this page at this very moment would hold this to be true. Unfortunately; everything in between these two slices of bread, is a flat out question of what and IF? What if you could make the big IF smaller? You of course can certainly make it larger, that's the easy part. Just spend your life everyday without a care as to what happens to yourself, your wife, and your children

And your loved ones. To leave your bag wide open, not taking an account for anything and allowing the chips to simply fall where they may is not only dangerous but a very ignorant way to think of life. I am very aware of the time in which we all live, and yes this society has fallen to depths of certain ruin slowly, but none the

Less surely. We all need to immediately focus on shrinking

Our IF, by taking the necessary steps to change our lives and the way we think personally. This will directly affect oneself, as well as those you love and care for. By utilizing everyday of your life, to something about the IF, is the beginning of change and understanding that, now is your time for action. Every second that ticks away on the Grandfather clock of life and death should be your reason to ensure or at least limit the uncertainties that can smack you in

The face with UN-preparedness for the IF. Do all that you can to become a more conscientious person no matter what your age is, there are no excuses for ignorance. Do not allow the inevitabilities to catch you in a deep slumber, remember that you are on the clock until you take your last breathing of oxygen. Who has an abundance of time to let go without any action or result? If you know someone like that, I'm sure that if you tell him or her of what you have read

They might have to do some readjustment of their thinking habits and living patterns. You can ease the big IF in your life by implementing and understanding what it is that you can do. There is action to take now! If you care at all for yourself and or the people you love you will and must make a full effort towards accomplishing the following:

(1) Contact your local Life Insurance agency or agent today. I urge you please do not delay, the price for

Not assuring your life and or the lives of your husband or wife and children from the big IF is all too costly. Who do you love? When we die suddenly or from old age whom that we love will be taken care of?

(2) If you do not have a Passport, go and get one ASAP. You just never know when your rights will be stripped from coming and going as you wish throughout this country in the near future. The uncertainties are far to great, what IF?

(3) Learn a Law within the judicial system, make it a practice to research this information at least once or twice a week. To empower you as an individual is key in this life. (

4) Enroll in at least six to eight units of college courses. It is unbelievable how much learning something can add to one's understanding and abilities of themselves.

(5) Parents! I urge you, turn the T.V. off. We are not taking enough time to teach are children. We have become a society, which allows for skin to be in and anything goes. If you do not sit with your children and understand each other's way of thinking, likes and dislikes etc. You will lose! By just doing these few small steps will enable, empower and guard you and your loved ones from THE BIG IF?

36. When Will We Start Listening To Learn How To Live

Honor thy father and thy mother, that thy days may be long upon the land which the Lord thy God giveth thee. Ex. 20:12 Did you realize when the bible tells you how to conduct your behavior in life that it also implies, when you don't obey what it says, the results you receive are the opposite of it's promises? Life brings with it some difficult experiences, such as marriage, and we have to adjust to co-exist in order for our future to be lived out in peace and quiet as we transition to a much slower pace of living with age, preparing us as wise counsel and support for our children, grandchildren, and the unborn generations. We have all shared in the passing of the mantel as our parents die and each succeeding generation is promoted to it's new position of hierarchy within the family structure or have you not yet noticed this natural phenomenon? When children become parents, by choice or accident, an adjustment must take place. Your world of play, fun. And adventurous curiosity is suddenly cut short, and the responsibilities of support, teaching, providing, thinking, planning, sacrificing, and hoping for a successful future for your children, enter your world and sleepless nights pondering how things became so complicated and the questioning of self and the abilities to make critical decisions that impact everyone. God knew what he was doing in establishing this order, but humankind because of it's education and self reliance has tried to escape this perpetual cycle of generations and families are suffering for neglect in following this basic institutional pattern for building better individuals and harmony as we move into new decades together. Mentoring is everyone's responsibility, but many of us are failing because our example has, self declared arrival of mature reasoning, our understanding being limited and shallow and in our pride, we fail to acknowledge history and more often fail to utilize the experience of preceding generations in our stubborn stand, which if clearly recognized, amounts to rebellion. We dare to say it's mine, I had it, I bought it or I work everyday, and think this declaration justifies dangerous and careless even neglectful actions and attitudes, and insult the very people that have given you life and provided and sacrificed to raise you to a level of readiness, not arrival, and push our older ones aside, indignantly and nastily, saying " I'm over 18, or I'm grown, I can make my own decisions, I know what I'm doing." This couldn't be further from the truth. One of the best indicators by which you can measure how you stand in relation to maturity and the ability to exist with others, which also in the same thought is the very information and example our children will emulate in their lives, under our instruction by example, is the way you handle money. Examine your finances, and if you can see a need to

99

improve, I guarantee, you've got issues that need serious attention and work to make needed adjustments. Most people ignore this barometer and continue on to eventual ruin, frustration and anxiety of being stripped of material acquisitions, many even get help, then repeat the very dilemma of this experience in failing to seek and utilize the wisdom and experience of older people. Well...where does this leave us, and where are we headed in out thinking? You think you can leave God our of the picture, you insult those he sends to help you, and refuse to humble yourself to the teaching of his word, and you want to live a happy and prosperous life doing it your way. Sorry...you've got a big surprise ahead and you won't be able to say you weren't warned.

Ec. 7:9 are not hasty in thy spirit to be angry, for anger resteth in the bosom of fools.

7:16 be not righteous over much, neither make thyself over wise, why shouldest thou destroy thyself?

8:11 because sentence against an evil work is not executed speedily, therefore the heart of the sons of men is fully set in them to do evil.

Don't think for a minute because it says man, or son, that it is being only gender specific. The bible is in context very inclusive in speaking to women also, when it is not specifically direct. Watch your children closely and remember the attributes in you that you dislike about the way your parents raised you, then watch your own actions and how you speak to your children, and remember the future will let you see how imperfect you were as a parent, and we dare to send our children to church while we return to bed...we're all tired, but church is not to baby sit your child, it's there to teach families how to succeed together. If you spent any time at all in church while growing up, you've been prepared somewhat by parents who loved you and saw it was essential to be there with you. How selfish and lazy it is not to be a part of your own child's spiritual development... you work all week because it is your choices that have determined your obligations and lifestyle, send your babies to daycare, then neglect time together in teaching them who God is and think you're doing your best... wake up! Your example is drawing an image to your child of what and who God is to you, and that leaves you responsible.

37. Momma...Momma's Boy

After you think about what I've written, then conclude your evaluation of this information I willingly divulge, because arrogance and confidence are on separate pages, and my confidence is not self-constructed, but realized through a value system passed to me by support from my mother, a Godly woman, and developed through a relationship with the Holy Ghost that has shaped my transformation and renewed my way of thinking. They say that good things come in small packages, and the biblical translation reminds us not to despise small beginnings. I refer to this thought being short of stature, but a demanding physical program has somewhat altered that label, reflecting the average person, as well, the exterior of a man doesn't measure the size of one's heart or his devotion to whatever he commits to. The bible instructs us not to judge a man by his exterior or the clothes he wears, but compels us to get to know the inner man, then make your assessment of what fruit he produces in his walk through life.

Momma gave me good advice as a young adolescent and it has taken me through many situations of temptation when my nature wanted it's way, but that voice echoing in my conscience, supported by her words, helped me walk away from destructive behavior. The simple message she impressed upon my instruction was to, "never get involved with a woman you wouldn't want to marry." Now, I admit to having made mistakes that violated that teaching, but even then, circumstances prevented moving forward with the " do the right thing principle", that governed my choices, but putting the cart before the horse has proven to be my downfall, and believe me, I have paid dearly for getting ahead of God's will or more specifically, sex, outside of marriage. A man's sex drive will skew his objectivity in critical decisions if it is undisciplined, and the divorce rate as well as the growing arena of unwed mothers and unfulfilled involvement reflects this fact. Psychologists agree that same sex parents have the greatest impact on offspring, but as I have mentioned in implication, " momma" was the parent that established a relationship with me, so, as a male benefactor of her values, some things in interaction with women, I had to learn for myself, and trial and error is, emotional vulnerability when a father hasn't communicated to his son what his wisdom in balancing relationships includes.

My ex-wife used to say, after her heart had turned from the marriage, that I was still a momma's boy, but I finally figured out that was just one of many approach attacks a mate will use in refusing to self-evaluate, and the fact that her extramarital affairs had skewed her thinking and her misdirected anger created any excuse to justify wrong decisions, bad behavior, and compromised vows. The echo of the words, "you're not my father", never comprehending accountability to family values, allowed for liberal misconceptions of boundaries that must be respected at all cost, but lack of knowledge permits erroneous beliefs and false values spread deceit. I was considered a drag and a square, failing to do drugs, and run anxiously to the party scene every weekend, while attempting to raise two male children and learning adjustments to domestic roles that marriage requires was never satisfactorily excepted as a contribution to her efforts, another false perception of processes that require patience and understanding. They say that what you do to catch a mate, you have to continue to do, to keep them, and in the first year of marriage, she stayed home and when I arrived from work, the house was clean and dinner was hot on the table. Well, it was a small studio, and minimal effort to maintain the home was required so our relationship was established on sexual intimacy and hot passions of desires fulfilled, not realizing the dynamics of change that come when a couple grows into a family and the success of material development allows increased responsibility. Expectations increase and social connections broaden and the small intimate world no longer is enough to satisfy the hungry soul. I continued to do what it took to get her, but the passion, for her, eventually, as it will for anyone building on just one aspect of intimacy, and presumptuously existing in emotional, intellectual, and spiritual needs by both mates will produce inadequate communication development and drifting apart will result, while the social attractions widen in every arena.

After the ideals of values and roles caught by observation of a productive marriage have been devastated, the reassessment of society and trends of careless lifestyles and ignorance in the dynamics of human behavior patterns must be improved through educated information and wise counsel in order for the individual to move forward in a positive constructive fashion, if compromised values are to be restored to healthy development, so that the future manifests in peace and quiet, along with harmonious community living. Toxic people, if allowed to influence your value system, will have the truth twisted to accommodate their destructive patterns that seem almost innocent in the early stages of involvement, but the path, just going with the flow, will continue to lead towards an undesired future of disappointment and regrets.

In 1987, after separation, which led to eventual divorce, my desire turned to seeking the truth of the bible, and allowing God's spirit to lead my life. I have been on an amazing journey of ups and downs, trials and tests, lost businesses, a home, a wonderful Corvette, emotional stability, even physical issues of health, loss of speech through vocal chord stress for two years, an uninsured car fire, and in 2003, the death of my mother, an almost fatal beating of my youngest son, and many other challenges with discouragement and question, but God has brought me through it all and left me amazed at his wonder of mercy, love, and faithfulness. As I wait upon his promises and hope for the future, the word reminds me that his steadfast love is new every morning, and as a mere man of flesh, he has forgiven me when I failed the challenges to endure the trials and testing of my faith, yet, my trust is still in God. I have been called many things, and many insults I have had to ignore, but the most amazing thing I have experienced is a pure mind towards Him. I feel the fact that in my sex life I have honored God for 17 years, since my ex-wife left, not because I am good, but because Christ died for me to give me this renewed life and opportunity to serve him, and by his spirit, I can do all things through Christ who strengthens me, and honor his commandments by the way he helps me live.

Present your body a living sacrifice, holy and acceptable, which is your reasonable service. It hasn't been easy, it would be a lie if I said there haven't been lonely and painful times of disappointment, but right now, "I am floating on eagles wings.

38. We Are Created In His Image With Freedom of Choice

We are always amazed when our dreams and wishes are dashed and battered against the shore by the storms of life. To think how well we started in pursuit of ideals and that perfect experience of fun, pleasure, and gain. Somehow happiness slipped out of our grasp and the painful experiences of disappointment and disillusionment replace the anticipated hopes of yesterday's morning sun. Even the bible teaches us that "weeping may endure for the night, but joy comes in the morning. Ps. 30:5". You ask, "Where is the joy that young lives dream...so generously promising?" Where are the songs of my youth, and the thrill of each adventure that made me quiver with chills of passion and expectation? We compromised our values for things we thought were good...often they were, but we missed God's best plan, his perfect will.

Gone with the innocence...so much scripture comes to mind, Ec. 11:9,10 -12:1...you have left your first love...and God promises you will fail because you built a foundation on sand instead of the rock, Christ Jesus. Now you understand! Our journey of life has so many unpredictable seasons that it can be a wasteful tragedy to spend so many years to end in a defeated experience, whatever it might be, that you placed your confidence in. Hosea 4:6, my people are destroyed for a lack of knowledge. What needless pain we bare because we do not trust God and his word. We harden our hearts and stiffen our necks to continue down destructive paths, assuming the bad will change or just go away, believing things will turn to good someday, just hang in there, refusing to submit to God and so we are ever learning, but never coming to the knowledge of the truth.

" Well, if you are God, why didn't you just make me do right?" "If I had made you like the animals or the stars I slung into the sky, you would have obeyed me because you were given no choice. But we made you in our image and desired relationship and worship in a faithful trusting fellowship that I might be glorified by my most precious creation. Your father, Adam, has given you an inheritance of sin and death from the day that you were born of woman. I sent my son to die that you might believe in him and inherit eternal life with us in heaven. I sent my spirit to you as a helper to lead and guide you into truth and understanding...but in your heart, you followed after your fathers and chose to do what you would in spite of my love for you. You declared you were a free moral agent perfectly able to decide what is best for you, and asked me to leave you alone to create your own purpose and destiny."

"But you are God!" " I can see that you are real!"

"I wanted you to believe by faith before this day and trust in my word as truth...

This test of life, you have failed...

You have made the choice...depart from me, I know you not!"

"Now you understand!"

By Errol V. Moore Sr.

Chp. 5 Poetic Communications (spoken word)

39. Release

Just got off of the phone
With my dad
I had a thought
In my head then laughed
That's when I reached to grab
This Starbucks bag
So I
Began to write this piece
It was a piece of heath
Meaning too sweet
Or better than Sho' Nuff
With cons on his feet
Yeah I can
Speak through my pens ink
Upon a brown bag
I say
Where a zucchini loaf once stayed
But now this bag
Has
Become a canvas
For which I can paint
My thoughts
My soul
Revealed and released
Like an open window
Welcoming the entire earth
To come inside for a while
Right this way if you may
Lend me your ear
Loan me your eyes
Lease your mind to me
For one moment of time
As I break silence
Like a fresh shaved Louisville Slugger bat
To a car window
No more holding on to
What was or what is
Gone is the lid
Over my expression

Blessed in a land
Where I can be free
With free hand
Short hand
Long hand
With no hands
I'd still write
Just look at all of these pen bits
From every clever thought or moment
At the height of writesmenship
My thoughts have to escape
Some how
Some way

--Errol V. Moore Jr.

40. Broken Silence

I'm way
Overdue for some mention
Tired of the detention
My bars are still in prison
Hungry I'm still sippin'
And crumb 'in
On some chippin'
Pieces and cheesy reasons
The industry be scheming
While the artist
Be breathing
On life support for seasons
Rocking shows
Under grievance
For some twisted
Agreement
Pockets be deep and greasy
I saw and
Let it teach me
Got paid for
Playing peachy
Then squashed it
Underneath me
By writing and releasing
I know it
Ain't all quiche'
Pearly white
And all happy
Sometimes
It do get nappy
But when the sweet
Gets crappy
Work on some new adapting
Fine ways
Make it happen
You can control it
Captain
Don't be molasses act 'in
Sap slow relaxing

Waiting for things to happen
Stop the head scratching
You need some inertia
Jackson
No more slide slacking
Backward reaction
Time keeps
Ticking and clicking
Now you the force action

-Errol V. Moore Jr.

41. Bring the pain

I was born
October 16, 1974
Fresh into this world
Little Errol Moore
A sickly child
Mumps
Chicken pocks and more
Couldn't digest the fat
Of simalac
I was intolerant to that
When relatives tried to hold me
Pinch my cheeks
And pat my back
I threw up
All over them
So they nicknamed me
Doo Doo Bird
I hated that name
In fact when I heard that
It really messed with my head
Yes it did
But I just learned how to accept it
I guess that's how my skin grew
From thin to thick
Even when my parents
Couldn't make a fix
Divorce is forced
The kids get that end of the stick
A family divided
Left to fend off life
In which if united
I would have had help to fight it
Just puberty and me
Please
I was chastised and teased
From a young boy into my teens
Bullied and sometimes beat
So scared
I even got on my knees

Like Superman to Zod
In fear of another human being
Petrified of the unseen
Left my courage
No chance to be
I wish I had a second chance to see
What I know now
I believe these things affected me somehow
The way I am is how I was
And who I am is all because
The pain

--Errol V. Moore Jr.

E.V.M.

42.   Back 2 the essence

That's where we come from
That's what we live by
That's what we've learned from
Life's pages let's turn some
In a reverse mode
Before you smoked your first bulb
Remember your adolescents
Growing up with no control
That's real as what you breathe
To under spoken to be the leader lead
Did you follow that breed
A brother man creed
Your city was the pod
And you were the pea
Or more like a pawn
On earth's chest board
Virtually 360
In your city being raised
That's your his story
Remember the yesterdays
Let me demonstrate thee
Searching through school ground hallway's
In faster frame rate
A minor black trying to develop a mind state
At the same time put you in a timescape
Through Time
Though Time
Wouldn't wait
You got to be raised
This isn't a phase
You must deal with growing pains
No room for debate
To urgent to translate
Where every move you make
Can dirty your life's plate
Let's take it back
Flip a page to determine your fate

-Errol V. Moore Jr.

114

43. Awesome so amazing

Mover of all things
Destiny's destination
Glorified by his creations
All mercy
Pure love
Sky master
Earth creator
I tell you no
Not one greater
All powerful
Yet graceful
Perfect and patient
The description easy
But one single word
Cannot define
Awesome so amazing
GOD
The prime of primes

Miraculous and outstanding
Provider
Healer
Breathe giver
Forgiver
Sin deliverer
Remover of pain
Distress and death
As if it were a mere sliver
Until no other choice
But to have faith is left

Mountain mover
Water rippler
Life giver to land and sea
Holy and purified
The beauty
The majesty
Awesome so amazing
Even the non-believers

E.V.M.

Must praise him
If not
They must be crazy
If they want to see the tribulation

-Errol V. Moore Jr.

44.   Another day at the office

Yeah
I got a job
A J-O-B
A just over broke
If you know what I mean
Who told these men?
To micro manage me
They talking about
Numbers over quality
Stressing me out
Why
Hmm
Can it be that I a black guy
Hmm
Nah I found out
They want clones
This isn't a military zone
Plus I pay my taxes
By then I'm tapped out
From my other expenses
Now you want raise
Health care
And my dental visits
All you talking bout'
Is padding your britches
While I work to the bone
Earning scars and stitches
I need a witness
Stand up
Time to resist this
Corporation Slave Nation
Trying to look innocent
Down sizing
Up sizing
Back stabbing
Lies tied to business moves
And alibis
As the economy wipes its tears
With stocks and investments

E.V.M.

That remains dry
Yet you still spend billions
Using technological advances to spy
Monitor and pry
In on your employees
Who have families?
Living from check to check
Just trying to get by
Why
All for an extra million or two
Do you really need that?
96% raise
Just to splurge
On another yacht
Fool
Mr. CEO
Or should I say Gepetto
Your nose is growing
Like that of the puppet Pinocchio
When will it stop?
No one knows
As you continue to
Squeeze us bottom feeders
Smashing our dreams
And giving us a false
Since of security or none at all
Not even a care or concern
For ones piece of mind
And family
Financial stability
No
Just the bottom line
Power to the company
And money over everything
Which definitely
Includes
You

    --Errol V. Moore Jr.

45.   2 close to trust

It was
Nine thirtyish or 10 o' clock
I was watching
Star Trek reruns with Mr. Spock
Then I heard a tapping at my door
That turned to knocks
I turned the doorknob
And unlocked the dead bolt
Standing in the doorway
With eyes black as coal
Beat up and bloodied
Stood my brother
"T MO'"
His pain shot through me
Right down to my soul
I said, "What happened"
He frowned up and said slow,
"The last thing I remember was
Stockton or Modesto
A valentine dance with lots of pros
There was this girl who needed help
She said her car wouldn't go
Do you know anyone here with jumper cables?
I was trying to be nice; I was willing and able
So we walked through the parking lot
I thought things were stable
I popped my trunk
Reached in for the cables and got stapled
Unable to defend
Man it could've been fatal

-Errol V. Moore Jr.

46. BEAUTIFUL

You can open up
You don't have to be
Stuck
Press your luck
Take a chance
Risk it
To lift it
Physically flip it
In order to get it
You got to grab
Sort of like a savage
Without foaming
For the cabbage
Cash can be a sickness
And we all have it
We spend it to look
Lavish
In order to stay mannish
Our fetish is satisfying
Our ego
Habit
It's like trying to erase
Paint from a
Canvas
When you're crammed
And force-feed images like sandwich
What's hot?
What's in?
What's not?
Man it's
The challenges
I can't stand it
Still I'm trying to
Have a hand
In organizing the planet
Aligning the stars
With my verse and my bars
I wish it stayed
Beautiful

When times got hard
Just make your mind up
Either you not
Or you are
Instead of stressing
Let's go spend a day
At the park

--Errol V. Moore Jr.

47.   Back to Rap
I used to hold it down
Back in the 90's
At your school campus
Is where you could
Find me
In the quad area
Without a DJ
Or microphones for MC's
Just straight vocals
And harmonies
You would ask the audience
Who has the beat
And off the top
A beat box would release
The crowd judged you
On style and speech
Either you got the props
Or it was plain and weak
Some cats could freak
Techniques amazing feats
Had people biting
The same verse
The next week
Hip-hop was alive
To even nerds and geeks
And it sure saved some
From banging in the streets
Those were the days
When rap brought the heat
Now I'm afraid
It's overcooked to a mesquite
We need to take it back
Rewind time repeat
The decade lost
80's to 90's

-Errol V. Moore Jr.

48. Both ends of the sugar cane

**Butterfly O' Butterfly
If it taste sweet
If it looks sweet
If it smells sweet
It must be
Just as sweet
On the other side
Besides
You've already sucked
The other sides
Sweet sugar side dry
No more need you try butterfly
You cannot hide
I see your wings spread wide
Far from the cocoon
You grew between the skies
Then you put me aside
For I was blocking the exit
To the greener outside
Don't let me be the
The window nailed shut
No
Go on butterfly
Here's your space to grow
There are millions of new things
Out there of which you can
Get to know
Besides
Both ends are sweet, right?**

-Errol V. Moore Jr.

49. Candle Shadows

Mo' rice would be
Nice you see
Tossed out
For the groom
And the bride to be
Over the broom
Make room for this
Symphony
Of love changes taking place
Between you and me
It isn't hard to let you know
How it's meant to be
Listen close
Brace yourself
Cause it's real to me
Clip them notions
Stop the questions
Take it easy
You're so elegant
A proper dime breezy
Girl it isn't all about
Your physicality's
I love what's deep in you
Measurements
That I can't see
With perfect patience
There's no need to get antsy
Your whole presence
Are the nectars of a blessing?
No doubt
I was more than just checking
You out
Of sight
I really want to know
If it would be alright
For us to converse mentally
As we dim the lights

-Errol V. Moore Jr.

50. Change

The fact remains
Even when you scrub it white
You stay the same
No matter your status
Or the circle's you claim
The image is circus like
Cages and chains
Change
Caught up in a social game
Trying to adapt
For acceptance
Into the frame
I know you wish
That it
Really wasn't this way
But it is
The truth
Does not lead astray
Change
No
This barrier is not ok
We're all GOD's people
We bleed just the same
So instead of skin hating
Let's run for it like Payton
One nation
Under understanding
Making
Change
For embracing
Differences
Respect each culture
We're all significant
Let's go
From the Delta's
Bays to Metro's
This is supposed to be
A country
United

We need a
Change

-Errol V. Moore Jr.

51. Choices

Fire to the flame
Now you burning
To get them wings
On your back
You must earn them
So do it to the maximum
Like Vernon
Get your cream
Get your cash
Money earning

Nah cat
Chill relax
You're too early
I know you
Want to fly
In eternity
Like them birdies
But your ways
Are all way
All to worldly
You know GOD
Don't play games
Don't jerk him

You have to walk straight
No herky jerky
There's law in land
So live it Murphy
Don't hate your fellow man
Respect is worthy
Do like your savior
Have some mercy

Don't wait till it's to late
Gurney Emergency's
Now your body's cold
Death comes soon
Certainly

E.V.M.

**I hope you hear
What I'm saying
It's a warning
The Reaper won't wait
Till the morning**

-Errol V. Moore Jr.

52. Destiny's Destination

When I die
I want to know that
While I was alive
I
Did what I had to do
What had to be done
Was did
That I
Used my guns
And utilized my reason
For my very existence
No questions
No guilt
Not a trace of old dirt
Nor footprints left behind
Like clumps of unforgiving filth
When I die
It shall be in GOD's time
Sent down from the heaven's
Written with perfection
Ordained to be
You don't have to ask
Why?
You see
When I die
You'll be just like me
There's no escape
From the destination of destiny
The order has never changed
Throughout history
So when we go
I pray we do it
In
Peace

--Errol V. Moore Jr.

53. Die2self

We're moving in such a pace
Living in a rat race
No time to take a taste
Slow down
No way
Time keep burning away
Trying to hold on to minutes
A day
When everything is instantly
So automatic it's hard to see
We barely have time to breath
24/7
360 five
Minutes is all we need
To smell the roses
And still compete
Can't you just feel the heat
Like a cop without his heat
In the middle of a robbery
We all like
Don't stop me
Blind towards our every step
Watch how you sow
Your rep
In the end you'll reap
What you thread
When it all comes to a head
Your better off
Better than dead
With regret and a pile of bread
Or a pot of gold you buried instead
So selfish is what they said
You feel the world
Is yours to get
So serious
For worldly possessions
So curious
To explore life
Like it's a pyramid

Are those wings?
Or simply it's
Your arms flapping
But the feathers won't stick
You're only human
So it's
Only natural
Where you're going
Only God knows

Could you see yourself?
On an island with no help
Only you and know one else
Where know one can hear you yell
Dry your tears from where they fell
Hold you tight
When you're feeling stale
Heart aching off the scale
Lonely simulating a cell
Doing time emulating a jail
You wonder just where you failed
Was it everybody else?
Or did you believe in what they felt
Why you got to doubt yourself
So scared
In fear of the belt
Of life and the challenges dealt
Let it cook you like a patty melt
It's time to shake you
Give him praise and know one else
Baptized trust his help
Come a new and
Die2self

    -Errol V. Moore Jr.

54. Don't Go

One thing I know
And understand
Without a doubt
I want to be your man
Not a simple sidekick or a fan
Don't push me away
Baby hold my hand
Don't be dry
Like the sands of Afghanistan
You send me swinging
You can call me Tarzan
But this loves no jungle
So why the racket and fuss
I ask God for strength
When we argue and cuss
It hurts me to see
That reflection of us
What is a relationship?
Without the trust
Sometimes there are reasons
For wrinkles and scuffs
I guess we're just human
Perfect not much
Lady so tell me
Are we dust or what?
I hope we can make it
Instead of just giving up

Don't Go

At times you treat me
Colder than snow
My mind gets all messy
Like a sloppy Joe
I tell you I love you
You push away
Tell me no
Why do you hold
Onto grudges so old

Without patience
How can anything unfold
The foundations still drying
I gave my family my soul
My seeds and my wife
Without ya'll
I don't know
Not on this earth
I'd rather be by the throne
With my father
In the heavenly skies
Just look in my eyes
See if I'm lying
If we slip away
How would my heart
Stop crying
Will you be there
Or are we truly dying

Don't Go

I don't want wedges
Between me and you
Where did our love go
Baby what can I do
Rewind time
When we first begun
In the fall back in 1991
A kiss in the park
Something like a dream
It seemed surreal
It was true love
On the big movie screen
I knew at that moment
Girl you would be my queen
When I got home
I wrote you this theme
Roses are red
And baby violets are blue
Together we were that beautiful
So what's the issue?

E.V.M.

Is it wrong of me
To be stuck like glue
Or the white on rice in love with you
I gave you my all
My heart is so true
I'll scrap to nub
To get my point through
Just tell me lady
The word done
Doesn't mean threw
Out of the window
No more nothing can do

-Errol V. Moore Jr.

55. Everybody's Heaven

Reach deep
Into the trenches
Of your body and soul
Find repentance
Cause life sho' can
Escape in an instant
Through death
Clinching your teeth
Like a dentist
I'm a sample
Use me
As a witness
My testimony
Place the devil
On my hit list
Today he tried to
Make me go senseless
But I prayed
And grabbed my sword
To stick him
His goal is to
Entice our flesh
With sin
The enemy
Never had power
Over the righteous
Tell him
Christ is your savior
He won't like it
This war is spiritual
You can fight it
Don't fall
For the pitfalls and vices
Or get caught
Between the clutches
Of a too tight grip
If you speak evil
Put a zipper
On your lips

E.V.M.

Then break down
To your knees
And ask if
There's a heaven for everybody

-Errol V. Moore Jr.

56. Find Self

I feed my flesh
Through my
Eyes
Ears
Hands
And all the rest
I failed
All the test
So weak
Was my defense
Can I confess
Who will hear me now?
When I digress
Be lead a stray
Or
Look further out
Into an empty mess
Will I blame others
For fruitlessness
Or answers uncovered
I beg and I plead
For black clouds
Not to hover
How come my time
Seems hard
And they get to have it
Smooth as butter
Where's my cheddar?
Where's my custard?
They rolling nice
And I'm broke
Flustered
Look
In the mirror
Just me
Not you
No other
So who could it be?
Why me?

E.V.M.

How come?
Who says I can't be?
I better find self
Before insanity find me
Reach into my own pupils
With thought
To balance out my gravity
Stop fighting me
Give my purpose opportunity
Max my potential
Utilize my minds ingenuity
Cause only I can
Do it
See
It's up to you to find
You
And for me to find
Me
No matter what
Your IQ score read
It doesn't mean a thing
It's not about brains
It's how you use
What you think
Have belief in yourself
And there's nothing you can't do
You can't lose
Place all the chips
On you
Say that you will
Say that you can
Leap negatism
Look now
You can move mountains

-Errol V. Moore Jr.

57. For you and me

We all come from
The same seeds and soil
With good intentions
GOD made us to be loyal
To follow his creed and believe
There was a time he had to
Cut off an angel who
Lied and deceived
All over greed
He wanted the crown
He wanted the heavens and seeds
Thus spawned Christ
Made of flesh like you and me
Born to a virgin
To save us the sheep
Under his wing
He would be accompanied
With discipleship
They prayed and drank of his blood
And ate of his flesh
The mission
To bring about his father's progress
To under gird the word
Upon the chest of his people
And he did it until his last breath
On Calvary with his blood and his sweat
Nailed to the cross
Mocked and kicked
Left for dead
But to his great glory
From the tomb was he resurrected
And all this for the sin of man
Didn't you know?
You better wake up
Before the tribulation come
Then it's time to go
For you and me
This we need to know

-Errol V. Moore Jr.

58. Golden Eggs

My life is like
A needle to the vinyl
An MC
Giving himself
Kind of like the hands
Of Lionel or Barry Manila
Across the keys of a piano
What I write I speak
Then it's told
Then shrink wrapped
As I drop doe
Do it like a salesman
As I slang this rap material
Dump it out until it's all sold
Put it in the universe
To GOD
For every rhyme I wrote
And boy I got jaws fulls
In a city where notoriety
Is something awful
That's where I come from
It's a must to pay your dues
Just to get some
While other keep playing
That same old
Humdrum dumb
Let me show you
Where hip-hop originality come from
See, I've entertained thousands in
Countless sums
Throughout many city's
They run
Like I'm a golden one

--Errol V. Moore Jr.

59. Dedicated to Henry "Pops" Theodore Francis

<u>"His Spirit Will Never Die"</u>
Son, Father, Friend, Grandfather,
Great-Grandfather
And provider to lend a hand
Plus a craftsman
Military Diagnostics
McClellan Air force
Aircraft Mechanic
He was an inventor
A creator
Who never asked for the credit
Ask, "Pops" to build a cabinet - or a table
Watch him set it,
With measurements to precision
He instilled wisdom,
A real reason to listen
He spoke stories of the 1960's
New Orleans, Louisiana
Catfish, bourbon, and a dance by the piano
Told me bout' bayous and crawfish
As well as how to keep it real, stay humble,
And give when you can
The truth is, it's all about family not,
The pursuit of being a rich man
"Pops", enjoy your days with God
As you walk upon heavens golden sand.

-Errol V. Moore Jr.

60. Good-bye Mom...See You in Heaven

I saw an angel pass.
I couldn't see her wings, yet...
I felt the wind as she breezed through.
A transformation...
A passing over...
From life, into life eternal...
As God's breath...
Returned unto Him.

He sent it out...
Only for a season...
A time to accomplish...
His purpose.

As I sought to grasp the vision...
That I could not understand...
I could not see her wings,
But...I saw her face...
Shining bright with glory...
Not death...
But life.

Into his presence return...
His gift of time...
His power over all life.

The Rabbi on a ship tossed to and fro in the tempest...
The men aboard run to him in fear, to find him asleep...
"Lord, care thou not we perish?"
He stretches his arms as he rises...he yawns...he speaks a command, a soft word to calm the storm...

"Peace be still"...and the wind and sea obey.
Turning to the men he questions their doubt...
"Didn't I say we were going to... the other side?"

God has not promise skies blue,
Flower stewn pathways all our lives through.

But, God has promised...
Rest, for the weary, strength for the weak...
Undying sympathy, undying love.
Do not stand at my grave and weep...
I am not there...
I do not sleep...
I am the wind blowing over the hill...
I am the bird rustling in the bush...
I am the stars up in the sky.

-Errol Moore Sr.

61. I give thanks

You opened my eyes
And when I cried
You dried my tears
Took away my pride
My Lord without you
My river runs dry
That's why I'm down on my knees
By the mountain side
Thank you Jesus
For your sacrifice
You gave this whole world
The father's advice
We are nothing
Until unto self we die
So I vow everyday
To lift your name on high
So when I see my enemies coming
To bring me down
No I won't run
I'll smile away the frown
Because of you Lord
I find joy in pain
For it's where I'm weak
I find true strength
So when I fall down
Like sometimes we do
I hold fast to faith
Cause GOD will get me through
Thank you Jesus
For everyday
You died for me
Now I'm gone do the same?
O' when the sun
Rises to the day
Awesome amazing
My Lord is
I must say
I need your tender spirit
Before I go my way

Please protect my love ones
Lord keeps them safe
Let thy will
Be done on everyday
Thank you Jesus
For the path you laid
Christ through you only
Can heaven be obtained?
I give ye' thanks
Now I can make it through the day

62. Dear Mary,

I was introduced to you in the fifth grade
My best friend "Cel" showed me
Where you stayed
The first time I met you
I was kind of afraid
Because your father had a long beard
And an orange face
Your eyes were as green as parsley flakes
And fools around the way nicknamed you "shake"
But as time went on we grew in different ways
From your love potency
I had to separate
Until I meet you again in the ninth grade
I skipped classes so that we could parlay
In the back on the blacktop is where we played
But this time when we were finished
My head started to ache
So I dumped you and left you alone
My eyes got red and I felt like a stone
You messed up my mind
Twisted my time
Had my GPA on the decline
My counselor showed my signs
I was running out of time
Until I found myself out on my behind
With no high school diploma
Mary, to be honest
I wish I never had known you

-Errol V. Moore Jr.

63. I need to know

The question is so simple
I need to know
If I don't rock the crowd
Who's going to show?
If I don't get a pound
Where did it go?
A question like who did
Ron and Nicole?
Sunny one minute the next
Rain flow
Why is death in a hurry?
To let you go?
Some swimming in gold
Some broke to the bone
I question it now
I need to know
Can you really
Clean a bad mouth with some soap?
Why do pipe dreams lead to a lost hope?
Is not caring at all
Really whatever floats your boat?
How can I be funny?
And still no joke?
Does a hidden message
Really mean that's FO' sho'?
Are you an exception?
If you're a Huckstable?
Been there done that
Seen that
No
Something on my mind
I need to know
Who has the master plan?
Do you really believe?
In what he can?
Or do you just pork off life like a ham?
Look all around you
Now open your hands
Them lines on your palm

E.V.M.

Unique for each man
The greatest creation throughout this land
So don't take a minute for granted
Your life span
I need to know if you understand?

-Errol V. Moore Jr.

64. It won't be

Step away from
That boob tube
Mix in a book or two
Get your mind lubed
Prepare yourself
It's going down
Smell the air
Chaos all around
Suicide bombings
But not in your town
Shock and Aw
You might as well say
When bombs fall
Collateral killings
Large and small
Men
Women
And babies
Playing with rubber balls
Operation freedom
But what's the real cause
Money is madness
Oil for blood
The conspiracy thicker than
Oatmeal mud
How you gone free a people
While still oppressing us
Establish a democracy
Out of sand and dust
Place billions in rebuilding
What you tore up
Turn around
There's devastation at
Your home front
But you don't care
That's the way of a demon
Steal, kill and destroy
Till know one is breathing

-Errol V. Moore Jr.

65. It's all on you

You can take dirt in the mouth
You can take hurt
Then smack the mess out of doubt
No use in lagging or leaning
Straight peeing and pouting
You were born to make noise
No more silence
Start shouting
Your grand folks showed you
How to move that mountain
Same thing when you have
No cash for counting
You use what you got to turn drops
Into fountains
Oats into meals
I know your headache ache's
And your body in pains
From serving "Caesar" and "Sam"
And them cats called, "Bills"
Down here on my level floor
Where dope and death meet
Isn't weird at all no more
Where fiends do anything to score
Some get high like a condor
We're products of poverty's trap door
Even if you move to the subs
You'll still feel the heat
From societal strugs
That's why I say
Stand
We stand
Do not budge
It's all on you

     -Errol V. Moore Jr.

66. Like a jungle bop

It can get risky sometimes
Tricky sometimes
Misty eyed like someone close to dying
Life is a matter of brakes
We're born into mistakes
In a world full of
Flaky Jakes and slithering snakes
The fight between dark and light
Is your soul your own?
So are you ready for an early headstone?
You better breakout now
Come on get away
Before you fall down
Gravity isn't free
This isn't a get away
This world don't hand out
Giveaways
Just a hard time
And too much weight on your spine
Is it worth a whole load on your mind?
That's why some
Crack way to early
They give up and resign
With no hope for oxygen or pride
Too many problems that surface
Not worth the fight
They lost faith
With nothing left except
Self-belief and bad hype
Living out there days and nights
Blind without sight

-Errol V. Moore Jr.

67. Lost It

Niggas be
Feeling like gorilla's
Snatching Chinchilla
From the rich
Then trade it in for some Scrilla
For Real a my Nilla
He a cap peela
Living in a world
Where low income kills ya
The environment is
Either you get slain
Or you become the Killa
Before them zombies
Throw you back in the Thrilla
Have you looking like a Feringee
Or Reggie Miller
Don't get mad
Get ten times bigger
Go figure
We can't all be Jigga
But that don't mean
You can't be a heavy hitter
You can be what you want to
Not what they whisper
Do your own thing
Flow with purpose
Like a river

    -Errol V. Moore Jr.

68. Luv's strength

A seed feel upon the earth
From the soils
Roots spread like wild veins
Filled with life
Filled with promise and hope
Born from the mother under
Now ready
Reaching for life above
Peeking
Seeking the sun
Moon and water
For growth
For evolution
Time ask
For patience
Please
Wisdom knows
Listen first
Then grow
Higher and higher
Forming and molding
Transforming into what
Will and shall be
Destiny's choice only
Is the intended
Strong powerful winds
Rains, snows, and even
Fires
Can't seem to bend
Brake, shake, or skin
What has purpose
Shall surface
Survive
It was written to thrive
No matter what
And why
Don't ask if
Love says good-bye
Know that

E.V.M.

If it shall
It will
If it cracks and spills
Truth
Just refills
When it brakes
It seems to kill
Understand
When loves strength is real
The stars above sing
Beyond the galaxy's
Dust, gas, and rings
Thru the heavens
It's signed thru eternity
Peace..........

    -Errol V. Moore Jr.

69. MC to rapper

To many rappers
Not enough time at all
To many actors
Diluting what we call
Hip Hop
The mere word makes
Your head bop
Peace, to all the pioneers
Who helped pave the way
To the top
The first 808-kick drum
And sample that got chopped
The first trunk that sold
Product out the top
The first executive
To say, "that's hot" on the spot
Plus we the people
Who keep it going
Nonstop
We all get props
We all go through it
When our peers get shot
Rest in peace
To the fallen in Hip Hop
The movement won't die
Thanks for all you brought
You really do touch others
When you spill your thoughts
Through a studio microphone
Then scanned
Purchased
Bought
As soon as the track hits
You've made your mark
Either it's good stuff
Or a refund fart
So take heed to the music
When you represent the art
Grab the microphone

E.V.M.

Flame it
Take off like a spark
Do your own thing
Through new waters you chart
Then cut through it
Just like a shark

--Errol V. Moore Jr.

70. My People

Community building
Lift up the children
Crack the division
Time for some healing
Let's get loud
Bust thru the ceiling
Tell them to reshuffle
The cards they've been dealing
We won't take it any more
Share them zillions
You can't pacify
The millennium children
We see the snakes
We know who's been stealing
The truth comes to light
With all your dealings
Man made greed
Got us living like Gilligan
A recession
Huh
How you think we've been surviving
Adversity
Like a buck we've been riding
Hanging on with one hand
Still we're rising
Our will like steel
Which thrives while climbing
Never give up
We just keep on fighting
And living what's written
To some it can be frightening
GOD almighty got his hand
On this one

-Errol V. Moore Jr.

71. P-I-M-P

Isn't he sharp
Real neat
Looks like perfection
From his head to his feet
He keeps his money roll
Crispy and creased
He's about collecting
Cash in the streets
He spreads feed
From beak to beak
His women for sale
Selling cheek between the sheets
Even though he has a wife
And four seeds
Who have needs
They need their Daddy
Not a PIMP
Who needs Furs and Cadi's
Heroine, Thizz, Crank and Weed
To keep his tricks feinding for weeks
Stilettos against the road
The blues she sings
And damn she's high
Higher than bat wings
What a tragedy
Pimps also pimp
Runaway's
And confused teens
They have big pipe dreams
That destroy their lives
Scared by the knife
Of hustlers, perversions
And a life of strife
That isn't right
You know that isn't right

-Errol V. Moore Jr.

72. Plates

**Close to edge
Like a slipping plate
It's only a matter of time
Before it breaks
The closer
We get to the floor
To meet our fate
Look at yourself
Are you a slipping plate?**

-E.V.M. II

73. Roots to Ropes

My people
Your people
Our people
From the root
To the rope
Of time and Yesteryear
To today
We are
What we were
Born through the spirit
Our dreams and hopes
Grew wings
Like birds we sing
So sweet with joy
Even though the taste
Was too bitter to enjoy
We still scale
And rise above
From the root
My people
Shed it all
From tears
To blood
From hatred
To scare tactics
Segregation
Holocaust
Voter Disenfranchisement
Lies and deceit
So deep
We feel it today
We are a product of the slave
To the rope
We are no longer strange fruit
Hanging from a tree
Not in this age of time
Yet and still
There's pressure
Around our necks

Because equality
And opportunity
Never meet
For more than just breakfast
Or a light lunch
The conversation has been converted
Twisted distorted and perverted
Tweaked into a delusion
Of a few successful minority
Over shadowing the real story
Of murderers and thieves
Who started father and son corporations
Built from blueprints and ideas
Not there own
Stolen twelve times over
From the coast
To the ships
From the trade blocks
To human livestock
Striped to the vein
Mentally and physically
Leaving a stain and a stench
Which remains stitched
Today
From the root
To the rope

--Errol V. Moore Jr.

E.V.M.

74. Silky Galaxy

Why does the rain
Start falling
All over my face
The sky's crying
Why does the moon keep shining
Straight thru my eyes
I'm falling
Why do the
Stars
Keep on falling
Right before my eyes
Drifting slowly
Cross the sky
While I lose my focus
It's not cool when you feel
Hopeless
You know we all need
Tenderoni's
For hugging and loving
You only
Something real no fake
Pepperonis
Either love me
Or leave me a lonely
Don't base me off sign's
And no Zodi's
In this galaxy
You're so silky
Outer space
You're so rare
Show me
You're my friend
Not my enemy
Coming for me
Slip away as you pray
Get to know me
I'm real
I keep it real

So keep it rosé
When I need it
Come kiss me only
In your temple
I dwell
And it's cozy
Soft and fine
You're my herb
Naturally
You haunt my mind
Your face is after me
Through the nebula
Love is like light speed
Loose sight for a second
Then there's nothing
Your gravity
Pulls
My yearning
Let's share the sun
Baby don't burn me
In your eyes I see comets
And warnings
But I'm struck
And I'm stuck
I keep soaring
Towards your
Horizons
And beautiful mornings
In this capsule
I've been saving
Storing
All I have to give
Now I'm pouring
My soul and my system
You're worth it
My GOD says
No one is perfect
So for reasons
It is
To be destined

E.V.M.

**On earth
As it is
In heaven**

 --Errol V. Moore Jr.

75. Sin

Behind the door
Between the curtain
Within the shadows
Of temples and chapels
Done on the under
Down under
No wonder
It is what it is
Sin
Not Just a word
I heard
Sometimes it's hush hush
Sneaky and dark in the dark
A
Rebellion against God the father
The creator
That's what sin is
Forgive me Lord
For I've bumped my head
Over and over again
On the same rock
Maybe next time my head will just
Crack or pop
Open like a melon against the pavement
As if the Sin is so good
It's worth the pain
Until the guilt came
Like a child to his father or mother
Cowering in fear
And respect
For wrong is wrong
We knew that when we stepped in it
Sleep in
Swam in
Danced and jammed in it
Sin
Or sinny sin sin
When it comes to a twenty-twin twin
Shall I come again

E.V.M.

Or will you stop running
Where are going anyway
There's no escape

-Errol V. Moore Jr.

76. Spirit rock

Lord
I love you
So I ask you
While on my knees
Please
Take this
Spirit of darkness
From upon my shoulders
Out of my life
Satin trying to take mine
He wants everything
Doesn't He
My job
My wife
My children
Ultimately me
Not to save me
But to kill me
And he's been giving
His best
Blows lately
Got thieves
False claims
Satellites and airplanes
Violating me
Trying to break the windows
Of my sanity
By stealing
My ID
Moneys
A few lyrics
Some poetry
And a few memories
Him and his henchmen
Those who dare not
Mention
You
Your power your energy's
Plus to add insult to these injuries

E.V.M.

Got me chasing the tails
Of these centipedes
Of time
Around every
Corner
Twisting me
Turning me and my mind
Against self
With malpractice
Self-surgery
To suck the life
From your body and soul
Rendering you
Helpless and vulnerable
That be the
Devils M, O

So run quick
Haste not
To the rock of the spirit
I know his tricks
Plus all his moves
I was down with him
Yeah
I was the fool
So I know how he operates
In darkness
Between the shadows
Of the unwise
Full of lies
Drugs, wines, cheap thrills, deception, and crime
But huh
My will be unbroken
I carry the legacy of light
Even when guns start smoking
Against me
I've seen men fall
From the same things
A sufferer's way
Isn't easy
This world is cold

Hearts frozen
Trying to get a grip
Is slippery
Extra greasy
Trust in man
Is so
Slithering sleazy
Trying to make since
Out of all this
No need to
Worry
Nor dwell on the stresses
Cause when it gets deep
I just lay it down
At the rock
By my father feet

--Errol V. Moore Jr.

77. Stay strong have faith

My grass roots
My grass roots
Steaming from the days
Of chains
Where sweat and dust
Turned to mud
Hands all sore in pain
Surviving off of
Pig brains and intestines
No paper
No pen
Books burning in the wind
Decapitated higher learning
They claimed we evolved
From the apes
Black man
You're to fast
You're too strong
Your mind is complex
They want you wiped out
Gone
Off the face
Of this earth
But know one
Can play GOD
It just won't work
I know it hurts
That we're so creative
And innovative
Jealousy and envy
Leads to hating
You have a choice
To play with the rings
Of satin
Your eternity
One way or the other
Is waiting
Don't get caught
Running from the sky

When tribulation rise
I prey your soul be
Baptized

--Errol V. Moore Jr.

78. WILLIE

Willie
You allowed me to be me
When confronted
With fears of not being accepted
By an upper-middle class of black folks
I always looked for you
A smile and a handshake
Brought about comfort and ease
Even when my nerves
Where in a jam
Or in a squeeze
Thank you Willie
For being grounded in realities
Never did you hold
What you didn't know of me
Against me
You saw this book's cover
And you
Knew these pages were not empty
My past might have
Lost track of direction fast
But you didn't care
You spoke words of encouragement
Which I took to heart
Right then and Right there
The look in your eyes
Taught me one thing
To care is genuine
And that goes a long way with people
Your impact in my life
Will never be forgotten
You were to me an original friend, "Big Willie"
Thank you for making feel equal

R.I.P.
Willie Register
"I'll see you in heaven my friend, Peace."

--Errol V. Moore Jr.

79. U don't know

Ahhh
A diamond
She's such a jewel
A ruby
Graduated valedictorian
A natural beauty
Aspirations for Broadway
And the movies

You don't know

No problem, no hassle
Her parents have money
Plenty
Flowing out of the castle
No scholarship needed for her collegiate ness
Not when you are born with a silver spoon
On your lips

You don't know

She's a fiend for hugs
Her parents never taught her
The difference between
Money and love
Affection and such
Plus they were so naive
About sex and drugs

You don't know

About the abusers and thieves
Which never prepared her
For the encounter
With this dude named Steve

You don't know

He used her up like ground beef

E.V.M.

Or a peppermint patty
She became a dorm room treat
Her innocents freaked by
Steve and his geeks

You don't know

She was turned out
In just her first week
She shot up dope
Stayed drunk
Snorted coke
Smoked out her college hopes
Now her parents should've known

You don't know

-Errol V. Moore Jr.

80. Words

A word is not just a
Word
It can stand as tall
As the flight of a bird
Or used to perturb
Word
I concur
Used like a
Bat or a knife
With just one slur
A verb
Word
The tongue can be
Heavy like a
Pile of brick like turds
Hit you harder than a
Serena tennis ball
Serve
Word
Often times misleading
Like a hooker in a fur
Stilettos, lipstick, perfume
Tail wagging like a feline
In heat
Purr
Or someone saying it
Not as blunt
I prefer
Word
Spoken as a token of respect
Sir
Mr.
Ma'am
Ms.
Mrs.
Word
Taken out of context
Between a clause and contractual blur
What I said is

E.V.M.

"I never had relations with her"
Word
On the corner
Heard on a curb
Ears listen for the sound
Of just a
Word
To the street with a beat
Like a ditty
In rhythm
Superb
With language
Lingo
Communication
With slanguage
Word
No need for
Radio wave tables
Fiber optic or copper
Cables
Word
The latest in IT
Can't possibly micro process these
When it comes to freaking consonants
Consistently
Word
The English diction
Never heard
Of the usage used
Traditionalist
Say they must be confused
Word
Mathematic with the grammar
I fuse
Between salt, oxygen, and spit
Scientific
To be specific
The articulant
Speaker
Of words
Word

Is it hard to believe
We
The ones you called dumb
Dirt for brains
Word
Can take the small portion
Of so called equality
And opportunity
Thru all levels of adversity
And still
Word
Able to
Metamorphosize
Dis and recombobulate
The very
Language you create
We recreate
With the breaking of the standardized norm
By pushing the boundaries
Of the mind
Till the walls
Crack and disintegrate
Evolving
Surpassing
Utilized throughout
All speech
Known to man
As the very last grain of sand
Reaches the end of time
"Good-bye"
Word

--Errol V. Moore Jr

81. Who are you

Was I
Not supposed
To show up
Because you were here
Is it your opinion
That instills fear
In those who
Care
Well I careless

In fact
I can give a rats
Gluteus maximus
Towards your pre-judgments
And your critical intent
What insignificants
Did you actually
Take the time to analyze
My person
Your assessments
Are but a reflection
Of your own securities
And apparently
You have none

Your demeanor says
Larger than life
Yet
Your arrogance
Paints a portrait
Of meaningless imagery
Perception and deception
But most of all
You hide behind
A need for attention
By acting as if you
Have it all

As if your name was Midas
And everything you touch
Becomes as flawless
As a piece of polished gold
With speed
Your so
Quick to turn up your nose
As you fold back
Into self
For more glory
Acceptance of vanity
And personal honor
Tooting your horn
Over hyping and gassing yourself
Until you become
A great big bobble head doll
Of self gratification
Succumbing to your own
Circumcised mind state
Viewing those
In and around you
As minuscule
Imps and ants
Under your feet
Below your unrelatable level
Which brings me to the question
That I feel I must ask you
Who are you?

--Errol V. Moore Jr.

82. Without you

Thousands of years ago
Across the earth and new lands
God took his hand and from dust he made man
Then put man to sleep
Pulled a rib out of his meat
From flesh and bone became Eve
The first mother to conceive
Thus spawned the seeds
Which gave birth to we
Thru the Lord and his chain of events
We receive and now see
All the mother's and mommy's
The strength and the beauty
The will to endure pain
Thru delivery
Giving birth to life again
Feeling Eve's pain
Mothers your so amazing
You always stick to the grain
Without you
Man has little chance to be sane
Mom
The very definition of the word sustain
Without you
There would be no him
A plain bowl of hot cereal
Minus the sugar and cinnamon
No mother's embrace
A women's touch
Or lesson to be learned
No order in the mine
Or manners
To politely take a turn
Mother always told me best
As the world turns
Be safe or get burned
Be late and get left

Be smart or you might
Come face to face with death

--Errol V. Moore Jr.

83. Within

When I speak my mind
I create an open door
Into my soul
My very existence
The all
In which I unfold
As dynamic as the mind is
There's not one molecule
Of flesh that can equate to
Or hold up against
The power and great complexity
Which to man remains unknown
No hypothesis can come close
Nor theoretic boast
Which claims key knowledge
To the omni host
I believe truly
Only earth and the universe know
Due to our handicaps as human beings
Only through death will we know
The origin of light
Spirit and life
Our very nature blinds us
Deafens us
And numbs us
From it's greatness
It's patience and it's
Unfathomable strengths
As long as our skeleton
Which is encased in flesh exist
From the glory the soul maintains
A distance
Within

-Errol V. Moore Jr.

84. Use me

I am a rainbow
Use my moods
My reds, my yellows, my purples, my blues
Use me
I am a chair
Sit with me
Rest
Take it easy
Read with me
Lean on me
Use me
I'm a trash bag
Dump all your garbage upon me
Use me
I'm a flower
Blooming and bursting
With pollination
Sharing myself
As a process for growth and health
For my mother
Nature
Use me
I am a hand
Hold me
Find it in my grasp
Comfort and security
Let me lead the way
Towards righteousness
Faith and love
Use me
Like the water
As I quench your thirst
For mental hydration
Let me cool your nerves
And calm your blood
Use me
I am a microphone
Speak thru me
Amplify your thoughts

E.V.M.

As I inspire your presents
With projection and esteem
For what it
Is
That
You must say
Use me

    --Errol V. Moore Jr.

85. You take my breath away

Every time I see your face
You take my breath away
For you there's no need
For deep recollection
I remember the first time
On my mind you were pressing'

I didn't trip
On how easily out of black leather
You were undressing
Or the numerous times
Many men plugged you into
Different sections

Nah, I guess
I didn't expect you to change
I just drew out the sound
With a palm for each ear
Was it pleasure or pain?
I couldn't listen to your amplified
High pitch range

You know what though
You did keep it real
You never lied to kick it
That showed me respect
Quick as one, two and three
Automatically you
Keep yourself in check
You even let me know
When your levels were correct

Baby no disrespect
But
Can I grab your neck?
Are my words in the form of lyrics
Enough to catch wreck
And blow up your set

E.V.M.

I know you still love this
You can't resist the way
I lower my lips with hands drenched
Forehead full of beads of sweat
As my grasp becomes a grip
Turn on you and it feels just right
You're taking my breath away

-Errol V. Moore Jr.

86. Trust him

Lift up your arms
And say with me
From coast to coast
City to city
To GOD
It isn't hard to see
How his grace
Anointed and saved me
I know it's so easy
To fall to defeat
When we sow bad oats
That we have to reap
But you need to remember
To drop to your knees
Pray for forgiveness
Leave your mind at ease
For real
If your heart is hard
Like steel
Here's a cup of water
Take this chill pill
Find it in yourself
Cause your
Spiritually filled
You got to fight for your right
To love and not kill
Even if it means
Them enemy human beings
Get off that same o' thing
And you'll see
We all get to taste the honey
For free
There's plenty of time
For your testimony

-Errol V. Moore Jr.

87. Today

Today
I woke up
Breathing
To be thankful for that
Is good reason
I opened my eyes
To the day
Today
Yes
I could complain
Lay up in the bed all-day
Staring at ceilings
Waiting for paint to peel
Of the walls
Crushing my will
Chance in now a waste
Taking the easy road
Down wallow street
To that hollow
Negative place
Where gloom and gray clouds stay
It's crowded here
In fact
I saw all kinds
Of people
And many of my peers
No wonder why
Nothing ever gets
Accomplished here
Misery
She loves company
Do I make myself clear
She gripes for nothing
Everything is on the
Down
Not one uplifting
Thought
Word
Or sound

Just excuses
And a thousand reasons
To hang out a while
And stick around
But
No I say because
Today
I am full of life
And vigor
Strong as a nose
Full of aged vinegar
For insight
Creativity and innovation
Today
I do have reason
Even when the wind blows
Hard with rains
As wet leaves from trees
Stick to my face
Today
I am action
Towards my dreams
Hopes and aspirations
Nothing
And
No one
Will
Stand
In
My
Way
Today

-Errol V. Moore Jr.

88. To grin and to bear

To lose or to have lost
I used to believe in the cost
To love
To share and give my all
Now I feel like giving nothing at all
For a man to lay his life down for ya'll
To have it thrown back at him
Like a hardball
Is it my fault
Or has fate
Faked on time
The sweet smell
Is now a stench
Harsh enough to make you cry
But clear your tears quick
Without haste
Show some gall
Even as you try
To face life's brick walls
With bare knuckles
Beat it to the red raw
Never let dead ends be
Dead ends and that's it
We do what we must do
To grin and to bare it
With tragedy and death soon to come
Maybe now
Only then
Will people see clearly how
What we value and hold most dear
Is right in front of your face
Take a look here
Joy and happiness is a treasure buried deep
So deep in fact if that's what you think
To look beyond what you already have
Is the reason why people are never satisfied
 We'd rather run a few miles uphill
Instead of walking a few miles downhill
Our sights have been blinded while

Chasing money, prestige and glory
Do what you must
But trust
You will in the end
Bare it all
But will you still grin

-Errol V. Moore Jr.

89. Stubborn Me

All right already
It's getting kind of late
I can't play fake
I know I need them fat plates
Home cooking
Soft pillows
And fat cakes
A cat can't lie
She rock a pretty face
The smell of her perfume
And a women's embrace
Plus I'm tired already
Of looking at my face
Starring in the mirror of my car
I'll go crazy
Out here
As storm clouds appear
Where's my lady
The rain starts to fall
Let's forget about who's
Right who's wrong
Contemplating
I'm a be a bigger
Man
Go
Clutch my baby
This negative attitude
Got a brother all hazy
How bout' telling her
I need her
No ifs, buts or maybes
It's time for making up
Not more beginning the breaking up
I went back inside
Entered the room
What's up?
Girl you still heated
Or can we find freedom
She said take off your shoes

**Sit them down
You won't need them**

-Errol V. Moore Jr.

90. Stolen chances

How deep does it get
From the clergyman
To the sergeant at arms
The prosecution and the defense
Even that typing chick
All the way up to that old oak bench
Where judgment is passed
Though black robes
Perpetrating hope in a coat
Pockets spilling over with mo' any
Swiss accounts filled with money's
From rich folks
Influential envelops
A sad hope for those who come crawling
With hard times and "Man, I'm broke"
The system is set up to
Cripple your neck and break your
Motivation and your soul
Yeah you're sold
Now aren't you tired of that same o' same o'
Po' Po'
Racial profiling
See blacks
Suspect blacks
With a procedural mind F*$#!
They cut up our character
To make us feel less
Than a man
Equivalent to a Nat
Now get that
That's enough to crack any sanity back

-Errol V. Moore Jr.

91. Young Women Are Like Butterflies...Until The Silence Speaks

In a moment of chance...
Life revealed an experience the world...
Desperately seeks to capture.
Almost wishing to put it in a bottle, like a potion...
To reach and pull it from a shelf...
To devour its fragrance in filling appetites...
That hunger and thirst in need.

You can watch a butterfly in its dance...
Fluttering lightly through the air.
It's colors brilliant...
Her flight like laughter...
Awestruck to possess it's beauty...
To capture it in a net...
Device needed to stop free play...
To control life in a jar or...
On a page in a book.
Can it then still dance?
Can you see its freedom speak?
Certainly it is still a butterfly...
Found in the letter B...
But the dance has been removed...
And no longer can the sound of laughter,
Be seen in its flight.

"But look!" There. Another butterfly!

Boy meets girl...
Her beauty, a quality inward and outward seen...
She takes down her hair...
Flirting like the butterfly dance...
Boy rushes in to enjoy,
To possess the pleasure in his eyes...
The splendor of her youthful beauty...
The freedom of her innocence.

Selfish nature in Man.
Soon, to enclose her in a jar,
To put her on a shelf...

E.V.M.

With many other conquests,
Not willing to share her life and freedom...
Beauty only to be enjoyed at his desire.
Looking through the glass jar frightened,
She wills no longer dance...

Now, the silence has spoken.

-Errol Moore Sr.

92. Metaphorical

See the beauty in the flowers...
Colors of the rainbow share...
The flickering lights of clustered cities...
In the distance flare.

Have you seen the smiles of people?
All different and unique?
Who share in conversations?
The other things can't speak.

The mysteries of God's creations...
We will never completely comprehend...
Bright stars spread all in the heavens...
With no apparent end.

-Errol Moore Sr.

E.V.M.

93. A Father

Those words
Still rest here with me
Confirmation over the telephone
"I am pregnant"
Hits the very core
Of every man who hears it
A sudden rush of adrenaline
Heart racing like Nascar
So fast
It penetrates your chest plate
Head buzzing
Body slightly numb
Do you feel me?

The reality of action
Through sexual satisfaction
In addition
Now and addition
No longer a crush
Or emotional condition
It's real now
Responsibility is here now
Just months away from new life
Which will appear
From the womb
And what always has been

I can still feel you
Under your mothers skin
Your growing everyday
I smile as your elbow
Nudges against my face
Every time I speak to you
Sing to you
Laugh and play games with you

I do this
As a gesture
A greeting

To let you know that
Outside of your world
There is love waiting for you

For you have yet to breathe
In my world
So rest my love
Don't rush into this world
Take it easy
Let God's will
Guide you first
I'd be blessed
Just to see your face
I pray deeply for good health
Your first breathe
And your first cry into life
Will I be the first person you see?
When you first open your eyes
Welcome to life my love
I am your father

--Errol V. Moore Jr.

CHP. 6   WRITINGS, JOURNALS AND AUTOMOBILES

94. WRITINGS / JOURNAL LOG (3.30)

Dear Friend

6/20/04

My most precious friend,

Today I went to the restaurant early because I had to return home in order to give my sister a ride to church, so I missed an opportunity to see you and maybe say a word, maybe even just a smile or a wave to say hello. I had been looking at an old picture from the 70's or 80's, can't even put it in a more accurate time frame, but it reflected my sister and her husband during the early, prosperous years of their marriage, and I wanted you to get a perspective on how life can change, and the physical and psychological experiences we live. We are suppose to gracefully metamorphosize into creatures of beauty, as life transitions from youthful clumsy mistakes and strength and beauty of youth, to wisdom, and maturity, eloquently revealed in improved processes of successful living. Unfortunately this imperfect world reflects many sad results of the destructive nature of evil and its very attempt, goal, and often victory, to steal our hopes and dreams for the future. I thought I would just take a little time to share my thoughts of the past weeks and days realizing the very words I have shared with you about making needed adjustments in life that are necessary to enable us to move on or just move forward. The bible says that "if you stay in my word, then are ye my disciples, and you will know the truth, and the truth shall make you free," and I have learned to rely on this reality of confronting my emotions and objectivity in relationships and those things in life we hold dear to us.

6/25/04

It's been a very difficult week, and I'm feeling so drained form the stresses of life, and the patterns we attempt to maintain in pushing ourselves towards our goals. It has literally taken these four days since I began writing this letter to return to writing even though I think about you on a daily basis. I needed a clear and rested mind when sharing my thoughts on paper, there is so much information we process in each day we live and the people we interact with on many different levels. Today I recognized something so unique about you that I wonder if you are even aware of your personality mechanics, and it makes me curious about the experiences of your life that have shaped you and made you into who you are. It seems regardless of how awkward any specific day has been in my exposure to learning your characteristics, somehow every new day I see you it seems like a fresh start, as though the previous day almost never was, in its clumsy attempt to understand human behavior. I wonder if your walk with God is so close that his spirit in you is revealing this special gift we all can somehow obtain or if he gave this treasure only to you. The bible says unless we become, as a child and trust God for everything, just like our natural children depend on us for everything, we will not inherit the kingdom of heaven. I have only seen this action demonstrated in children, until now...how quickly they forget the confusion or issues of yesterday and life in the joy of innocent relationship at the present moment. It's a beautiful gift of forgiveness in realizing how imperfect we are, and the ability to overlook those peculiar ways that I think perhaps the pains and tragedies of life have caused us to react to in human interaction.

I have learned as a father, in observation, to discern and understand how human neglect and presumptuous lifestyles can damage a child's emotional growth and in the attempt by that child to correct his pain, he will build walls of anger and hide behind them in insecure places that seem safe when confronting challenges that life presents to enable them to grow in confidence and self-worth in multiple arenas of development in knowledge, and personal interactions within his sphere of peers and societies social adventures. All children seem especially disrupted by this lack of paternal or maternal involvement in nurturing and building confidence in emotional and spiritual characteristics that are critical to a child feeling acceptance, affection, approval, and safety existing within his environment of life. Boys often act out in anger, destructive patterns, and violence, reflecting the fact that 1 out of every 75 males is incarcerated in penal or correctional institutions. Girls also reflect this neglect by a parent in their spiritual development resulting in misunderstood emotional needs, leading to the pursuit of mature experiences prematurely, in the cycles of life, and our children are cheated out of years of normal development opportunities, and rushed into the mainstream of life with adult dynamics they are unprepared and unequipped to contend in, therefore, you see a high poverty rate among young unwed mothers, doomed to this escalating crisis of experience. Some even take on the dynamics in destructive forms and anger patterns similar to the violent male issues.

It is refreshing to me when I meet someone who is conscious in concern for their child and priority is not lost in self-indulgence, neglecting the needs of the child, but focused on the child's immediate needs as well as projected needs of the future. The scars of life children, who all become adult people, but not always mature rational and prudent, must endure is real and the pain created when left to feel unloved and unwanted, perpetuates society disorder at its worst quandary. Hurt people...hurt people, and while a lack of knowledge in spiritual matters escalates, the sad stories of destroyed lives and families continues.

If by chance you wonder why I try to be concerned and will often go an extra mile to do small things for you, I realize we must make a difference somewhere in our world. You have been open and receptive to me, maybe even more, the Spirit of God we share as believers, is a wonderful concern for others when we see a need, and maybe that example demonstrated before others will give them an opportunity to think out of the box life so often puts us in. The bible teaches us to be kind to everyone, but is says especially to those of the household of faith. Many of my pains in life resulted from the years of life robbed from me without my sons living in a home with me, and the disappointment we experience when our love for our children is hindered by s selfish companion and their agenda of evil shallow choices. God has proven he is faithful, and even redeemed the years stolen, just as his word promises, but I have a passion for building into the lives of others that this world system is deceitfully attempting to destroy.

09/04/04

I didn't know whether or not I would continue writing letters since my wishes have always been to share special times with people I consider to be important to my experience of living, but our lives seem to continue to move at such a fast pace, the precious moments of opportunity to share reflections are brief periods squeezed between how we prioritize what we value as essential or relevant to our purpose of each day. Between work, pleasing all those people you really don't even know, and there's just one you, school, raising your son, trying to incorporate a little time for anything you enjoy as an outlet, preparing mentally as well as presenting yourself professionally in these arenas of life in simple ways we dress and even the time it takes to commute between these ventures, we are always moving and the day has ended while our list of things to do seems to continue to increase. Just being able to get an adequate nights rest without worries and concerns of doing your best and satisfactorily meeting expectations of others as well as our own self-critical standards, sometimes we can feel overwhelmed and I can understand how you could simply cry yourself to sleep. It would be nice just to hear someone say everything will be all right and be reassured your efforts are appreciated and know that you are doing a great job, cause you know you are doing the best you can under the circumstances currently present in your world. Don't even talk about making the bed, mowing lawns or cooking dinner, school clothes, oh, and I've been meaning to go see a sick relative or close friend and there just isn't no more time to do it all. We are in a pressure cooker and it can be hard to discern who is for you and who is against you, cause everybody wants your time and attention and you can't hug them all, giving away assurance, when you know you need a hug to receive assurance that someone cares about you, not always for you. I can't even tell right now if I'm venting for you or for me, cause this has become the lifestyle we encounter that can leave a person vulnerable and wide open to disaster cause you can't do everything yourself and you don't know who you can trust with your emotions and feelings. Sometimes when we think we are being strong, we are fooling ourselves, that's why women cry and men crack under the pressure and escape to addictive behavior. Public interaction is a learning field of choices and exposure to wanted and unwanted involvement and being sensitive to one person promotes desire in others because everyone has issues, and life has many victims living in great pain.

Life is so funny...our experiences are at different points in life for a reason, and we need each other, but we have to learn and understand for what purpose. People begin to attempt to understand, but that is only the beginning of a process it takes to see the whole picture in a complicated society that has lost its vision, values, and direction. Gina made a comment boldly and openly, directed about me, and whether in humor or conclusion, based on inadequate information, she said I was running a male escort service, and in my efforts to understand how she arrived at this erroneous conclusion, she accused me of being a gigolo, because I commented I could use deductive reasoning to speculate on her hypothesis, but the margin for error would still leave me inadequately informed as to her comments about...my life. If you see a person 5 times a week for approximately 45 minutes to an hour, how then do you determine the remaining 163 hours per week in that person's life you did not see them? I could not take offense to her comments because I know there is a lack of understanding in her perception and thinking, but what if some bystander hears her and believes what she said...what have I become in that persons mind if they happen to see me somewhere around the city with implanted information to process, and inappropriate time and involvement to know the truth. Have you ever heard something about someone you didn't know and wonder if it were true? If I were living such a lifestyle as that, I sure would be rolling in a luxury vehicle of some kind, not in a 2001 Ford Escort. Common sense! I even thought about my small effort or comment about my son to Shanay...couldn't anyone reason that I liked her professional presentation and graceful attributes, but I don't know her to actually warrant a serious pursuit of match making. My son, I know. He is a handsome young hard working Black man, with 3 years of military service and immediately upon leaving the Army, he has maintained a job he has faithfully performed for

3 years...he is a young man seeking God in his life, he stays in excellent physical condition, is an outstanding athlete, and a sensitive man with hopes of being a good father and husband someday in the near future, something any prudent woman would want in her life, but it didn't offend me just because she said no to your inquiry of interest by someone, and I didn't expect her to understand instantly because life has choices and options. It was actually a compliment to her, but as you know everyone doesn't know how to receive one, because my son, I love, and wouldn't want him to be with just any kind of woman as he looks to build his future even with those he chooses as friends. You saw the picture of my other son and his beautiful wife and children, that's what my hopes are for any couple or friends that take a relationship to another level, which life has proven is the best formula for potential success in the joint effort of a man and a woman.

Wise counsel is critical to the success of any plan or goal in life, especially in considering a person for marriage, but too many people are getting counsel from sources that know no more about life than themselves and pretending to have answers that only time can bring through experience, is a formula for failure and disaster. Its ok to say I don't know something in life, sometimes you're actually not supposed to know certain things, but then in being responsible to yourself and to others under your influence, answers must be sought out in making correct choices in critical situations. Communication is a skill developed through the use and application of wisdom in interaction with people on every level of life, and failing to build on more than just shallow conversation, is not truly communication, and will limit the potentials to learn and hinder our ability to meet the needs of those we truly love and build successful efforts and goals.

That's what prayer is...talking to God about every concern of life we have. He wants to hear our thoughts of how we love him and he will bless and prosper those who are sincere in heart. The bible says in the book of Hebrews; found in the New Testament, that he speaks to us today through his son, Jesus Christ. How?

In the beginning was the word, and the word was with God, and the word was God. John 1:1 Read the bible and learn whom Jesus, the word, is.

09/20/04

I find it interesting that you would say, "maybe you don't want to know information about people passing through the business," and possibly it could be easier for you to avoid getting too close to people in an attempt to shield yourself from the reality of our world, that is full of pain and disappointment, and create a small bubble of safety and escape with select individuals that offer similar criteria for bonding and personal interaction. The bible even says...where wisdom increases, pain also increases, and we want to live out comfortable lives where everything is perfect, almost closing our eyes to the suffering that is a real part of life. Jesus told his disciples when Mary, the sister of Martha, and Lazarus, had broken the expensive bottle of perfume and washed his feet with it and used her hair to dry his feet, when they were complaining about her actions that they considered waste, "the poor you will always have with you", reflecting the increase in need when they are addressed, but the point was this critical time in history preceding his death on the cross. At this moment expense was not a consideration, but his preparation for crucifixion was critical. So there are some situations in this world we can't expect to eradicate in this life. I can remember when I recommitted my life to God in 1987. I literally was floating in the clouds of heaven and the freedom I felt from a miserable 10 year experience in a declining terrible marriage was removed form my shoulders that my legs could no longer carry, So I know what it's like to fantasize life's realities and I did that for almost 10 years, until my feet finally touched the ground and God let me see that my purpose wasn't just about me. He was making my experience useful to help others and without the suffering and hurt I had lived, I would never have become useful to Him as a vessel to touch the lives of other struggling people.

Friday...Today I did almost everything opposite of what I normally do. I slept until 1:pm, and headed straight to the gym for almost 4 hours of continuous running on the basketball court. Finally a little after 6:00pm, I headed home to shower and take a brief power nap, about an hour and a half long. I woke up and went to ...where else...I-Hop, my first meal of the day, and stiff from the length of activity decided to just go home and relax and watch a little TV, which bored me quickly and I fell asleep under the cool breeze of a fan at the foot of my king size bed. You know I was stretched out and knocked out. About 1:00am, I woke up as clear as a bell, I prayed for family and friends, in which of course included you, thanked God, and then I needed something to do. That's when I started working on the painting, and hours passed before I even realized it was almost 8:00am. What's so unusual about that night that I hadn't even realized, it was my mother's birthday, Sept. 17, and I hadn't even thought about it after all these years of honoring her, and many times, I would send her flowers, but now my emotions and intellect seem so much deeper in things that are spiritual, realizing almost one year and a half has past since she died and my inspiration to paint again seems rekindled. It seemed so peaceful as the new day began, and when I came in everyone seemed to be so pleasant and friendly, so I was moved to be grateful that someone else might enjoy the overflow of my blessings from above. After I sent the flowers and again returned to the gym for another very successful performance on the basketball court, I returned home to shower and received a call from one of my sisters to come over to have a fresh pot of Gumbo, which needless to say, delighted my appetite and redirected my tentative plans to go visit the friend that works at the Stock market, and my sister and I sat around reflecting on the family and issues of life we daily experience, as well as many past memories of others that have come and gone in our lives. Sunday morning seemed so different in the restaurant. It was as though the atmosphere was full of anxiety, with the exception of Shanay, and the moment you took to speak about the flowers, and to wish me a good day as I left...my observation of others was very uncomfortable.

I had shared the story of my mother's date of birth and the painting with one of the men at church, and he in response, shared this story with me. He had been married for 10 years, and had always made excuses for not wearing his wedding band; justifying it by saying he works in a lot of mucky substances on his job. He said the Holy Spirit had whispered to his heart to get his wedding band and put it on, so he obediently followed the prompting. To his amazement, immediately his children noticed he was wearing it,

And upon his wife noticing, she commented that she had been praying all those years for him to honor his vows by wearing it, but she didn't want to nag or pressure him by complaining.

I went back to my sister's house for more Gumbo after church, and one of my 13 year old nieces was discussing tryouts for basketball, so as I began giving her instructions and tips, it led into further conversation and she revealed that she loved to write poetry. So I asked her to share some of her writings, and was amazed at the gift she possesses for creativity, but her deep thoughts are to mature and intimate for a 13 year old. Her father just married, and was never married to her mother, and failed to inform her of his decision leaving her to process adult actions of emotions and complicating her lifestyle, not including her in their living arrangement because of other children in the household. To even complicate things further, she was just forced to return to Sacramento form another city where her mother and new fiancé' had no provisions for her to live with them in their new plans. A precious child looking for self worth, validation, and belonging to a family unit, with gifts and dreams, and neither parent considerate enough to make their child, the creation of a union once based on "love", a priority. The principles of the bible are still true even when we fail to acknowledge them as governing our lives or do we just see our children as consequences of bad choices...the two shall become one flesh, that's what each child is...man and woman connect, but the children are physical reality even when the parents go separate ways, and the spirit of that child still needs to be loved and developed. Too many children are growing up along with their parents, that is why they are so mature and provocative, and adults seem amazed when they make comments beyond their years of experience, even at times being more objective in assessment of real issues, not yet messed up and polluted by compromises of values and principles.

95. WRITINGS / JOURNAL LOG (3.31)

<u>A Hitman Story</u>
Soiled with sin from straight out of the pen
Into a Benz, black on black with gold trim
Diamond dust sparkling rims
With windows layered in tint
So that there's no seeing in
He felt at ease with these men
Who were considered as friends?
Clean cut chins with their Goodfella grins
Body's dipped in Armani tailored skins
Tapered to excellence
One of the men said, "Excellent
Just as we expected,
This is the spot" "Put on this uniform and
At that door you will knock"
"And from up out of this box
Reach beneath the Styrofoam rocks,
Revealing a glock then unload on this cop"
"Give him what you got until he's breathing not!"
"Then there by those steps,
Over there to your left
Will be a getaway car
The driver's name is, Jeff"
"So when all is complete lets say around six,
Jeff will take you to this destination
Where you'll find this chick"
"Who has a fetish for convicts
She goes by Mrs. Thomas"
"She stores grade a arsenal
That surely will astonish"
So after the slaying
Serious business no time wasting
At six O' clock sharp Mrs. Thomas was waiting
Everything was to caper upon arrival
She handed him a glass of ice water and a rifle
And said, "Here take these keys to this black Celica, downtown
At this address lives one Angelica" "She's the daughter
Of the governor, Angelica and the governor are close like replica's"
"Now go take her out!" "And then take this route, off

205 ditch the car and be out!"
"Like the unseen, you know the routine
By the way you'll receive 50k
When your getaway's clean"

-Errol V. Moore Jr.

96. WRITINGS / JOURNAL LOG (3.32)

LETTER TO EUGENE REDMAN, MY BIG COUSIN. LOCKED UP FOR LIFE WITH 3 STRIKES FOR DRUGS AND A PROBATION VIOLATION.

Dear Family,

Long time no hear. This is your little cousin Errol Jr. I've had you on my mind and in my heart family. I would like to let you know that I never stop thinking about you and where you are. Damn Gene, I wish this backwards-judicial system untwisted its unrealistic and conniving grip from your life and many other brothers out there. You're my flesh and blood peoples. I love you with all my heart, soul, and compassion the Lord has blessed me with. One-day family, I believe you will see, smell, and hear **FREEDOM** again. I will continue to pray for that very day. Big cousin I ask you, but, already know your faith is with GOD. He is your only light in the darkness you have to endure. Never ever give up on his energy, wisdom, will, and strength. You are not a number folks; you are not just another black face incarcerated. You are not just another inmate or statistic. YOU ARE A MAN, GODS MAN. Your family loves you and cares deeply for you and yours. You have seeds out here in this world that have to be raised, nurtured and taught right from wrong. Your little queens will make mistakes family, but as long as they find faith and know you love them and their family loves them they don't have to run to confusion or weakness. They can run to their family because that's where it starts. I'm sure that you have dissected your situation to them, and have taught them how crude this world can treat you, and what they do to human beings that don't deserve to be locked up some damn animal. It hurts me Fam. Just to think about the talents and wonder men in this world can take away from another. You know what though, all is not lost it only looks that way. I'm not going to sit here and preach to you folks.

I just want to express my deepest feelings towards you my flesh and blood and the anger I have for your situation. Well peoples, I guess I can say I'm doing all right. I got a job or (Just Over Broke), two baby girls one seven named Mariya Denise Moore and the other five named Minyon Deanna Moore, a wife named Cenne' Moore, and a love for music and performing. Yeah, I still get down you know, I won't quiet till I hit. God, got my back folks, to see me thru, and I hustle my gift to the fullest. It does cost to get everything I need to push my words to be heard, so I keep the faith strong and continue to believe it to be possible.

Eugene, if I do blow up or somewhere around there, believe me Fam, I will break bread for you to any measure for your freedom. That's all these tight suit wearing attorneys want, that's all the courts want, that's the ultimate bribe tool, cold hard cash money green face white men on paper cut outs. Can you believe that Fam. How in the world a piece of paper you can rip in half, burn, crumble, lose, and give away mean so much to many and do so much to get things done right. It's a trip when you break down things and decipher between what is important and what is not in life. I hate money folks. You might be saying what? But, nah man I mean that stuff makes this world what it is. People on the street no food, no heat, sick and what not all over not haven doe, people robbing and killing for that, somebody right now lying to their parents to go buy some get high what ever high that my be, somebody sitting around the house with no phone, no a/c, no lights, spoiled milk and moldy bread, cause they spent there welfare to the max and can't pay bills on time. Kids running all over the place, half of them they don't know what time they get home. This pattern screws the whole family bond up, no respect over doe, people using sex to get doe, hoes hoe for doe, and pimps primp for doe limp on street corner glimpse for doe. I'm just tired of working for doe, man everyday trying make things cool for my girls trying to stay on top of this materialistic society we tapped in to. I've seen big money before that's way I don't trip off the stuff. I realize the only real significance it has and that's to pay off other people and their hustle, credit cards, school loans, traffic tickets, (state, federal, and housing taxes.) All for what?

I can't sit here and make my world out like its all maggots, but it's not. I'm blessed cousin. I got my health strong, my little diamonds, a wife, a just over broke, a car, I own a duplex starter home, got food in the fridge, and loving people in my life. I don't take any of that for granted. I'm blessed and humbled by Gram and Pops. God rest their souls. They taught me how to appreciate life, the small things. They gave my enough insight on how they came up and what they went through to humble just about anyone when you think about it. Pops and Grams loved you as well Gene. They were good people and now they look down from our Lords kingdom and pray for us, watch what we do and us. Also, family you have a tremendous supporter in your moms. My auntie loves her sons so much all ya'll.

I remember back in the day when Terrell and me would be with my moms or dad and we would be driving down 47th Ave. Right on queue me or T would say hella excited "Can we go to Mikey and Gene's, can we can we!!!" I remember that like it happened yesterday. While we're on this nostalgic journey you might not remember Fam. But I used to mimic you all the time. You would come up with some words or a phrase and I would take what you said and use it. I remember when you used to say "get off it" in such a way that it was slang, you used it instead of saying stop or quit, you would say "get off it" or "come off it" one or the other it has been a minute though folks. So in closing I'm glad this letter has reached you and you now know were I'm coming from and pieces of what I'm trying to do in life. I just try to stay humble, I thank GOD for the air I breath, the ability to see, touch, walk, run, laugh, think, and all the little things we able to do that we don't think twice about because it's just natural to those who have and those who don't. I love you peoples. And I hope to see you soon…

Your cousin,
Errol Van Moore Jr.

P.S.
How can I send you some music?
I want you to peep out your cousin. Peace… God Bless You…

"LIFE IN JAIL IS FOR MURDERES, NOT FOR FATHERS AND POTENTIAL PRODUCTIVE PEOPLE OF SOCIETY." -E MO'

97. WRITINGS / JOURNAL LOG (3.33) LETTER TO QUINCY H. FOSTER "QUEE"

With love honor and respect Quincy "Quee" Foster,

What's up Q, man it's been a minute brotha. I dropped some rations on your books while you were at the county in Sac. I stood in line to come see you but; time and life drew my patience tight so I bounced. I really wanted to see you though folks. Man Quee, I can't really explain to you how I felt when I saw you on the news brotha. I just remember being hurt, kind of lost in bewilderment. I was like "nah man damn" because I didn't want to see that shhhhhtt!! To happen to you folks. They had you all over the news, channel 3, 10, 13, 31, 40 I mean every channel. They called you the "Grenade robber" and boy did the media eat it up for a while. It really gave them something to talk about besides the weather. Q, I respect and hold you close in my heart people 4 life. My Dogg, I knew that night we spoke for over 4 to 5hrs. In Greenhaven that there was something my soul, or my conscious was telling me to do. I wish there was something I could have done to see into your desperations my nig. Quincy, I love you peps. You always were like an older brother to me, one my parents never had. We learned a lot from one another I feel. Did you know that GOD places people in your life for a reason? We don't know why, when, and how but GOD knows what he's doing. I still say I wouldn't be where I am today without your impact, presence, or existence. I believe Q, that one day my peeps that you can have a second term at life, a second understanding, and second opportunity to find peace in your heart, mind, and society.

--Broke into a rap just writing and thinking about our past Q--
You never had it easy Q\
I never knew your moms\
But I always knew \
That you were always my nigga\
Searching for the truth\
Sho' did have it hard
To survive as a youth
You lived with your grams and aunties
When I meet you
Milford St., Sac town avenue
West coast soaking in the Cali bayou
Young cats Quincy Quee and Easy e
Cross 65th there was Ron B

E.V.M.

Plus remember the two Eric's, little pat and Derrick
Damien, Big Mark and his parents
Back in the day my community
I got to share it
Growing up as urban youth
Sometimes you inherit a scoop
Of bullshit before you reach High School
Ask me something
And I'll throw you a bone
Raised in the Gang culture and drug zones
Now throw in gun culture and my nig its on
So who would you turn to
In this type of condition
You better have a bible
And some good wisdom
Plus a proper box of
Street ammunition

For you Q, you can have it my love one. I wrote it for you to spit it to some cats in their peps.

Everything is going cool though Quincy. My girls are getting big. Mariya Denise Moore, she's eight. Minyon Deanna Moore, will be 6 in October you know how us Libra's do it. And Cenne', she cool man, just growing as a women and keeping her family moving for better things in life being a mom. She is a good mother, person, and friend Q. I just thank you and LaShonta for being in love so that, what I was talking about earlier, "GOD places people in your life for a reason you know". Yeah Q, everything blessed people's. I'm still at this music as you can tell but I'm just putting everything I do at GOD's feet man. That's all you can do Quincy, put everything at the foot of the Lord and let him deal with it. We need relax our minds away from this world of greed, murder, oppression, and devils. It's a true spiritual war out here, and I know in the facility you are in that fight is a lot heavier my nig but, Q, don't let anything every in life break you, but who am I telling. All the adversity that you have had to and are dealing with now is more than I could ever probably take. You are not dead until GOD says so, so until then my peps build. Build for self, build for future, open your minds eye and find wisdom. Seek it from GOD Quincy. Anything your heart desires is with your creator. Man, we didn't just drop out of the sky, or crawl from out of the ocean. We are the many faces of Jesus Christ and the father GOD my nig. We are strong in spirit, original man we are Quee. Find you, I know we are lost as a people right now but my nig find you. When you do that you will be able to capture what GOD has for you. And believe me Quee, there is something GOD allowed us all who are born to become something. God gave us life, to be alive my peoples. I prey that you remain strong and forever seeking to find wisdom. I need your help when you rise Q. My fight is for the youth, for this decaying generation my nig. GOD has placed that as one of my task in life to save our youth and become a difference maker for them and there future. Here is a copy of something I made up, as like a Non-profit type business I would one day like to create. I call it Let's Build, and maybe this might inspire you to maybe help me in the overall plan for this organization. Maybe if you have insight and writings or experiences you can get off your chest that could one day help change another life. Let's recover our youth Q. Let's not be side watchers, let us not sit around and allow things to happen around us. Let's be happening, let's be the ones doing not watching and waiting, nothing ever gets done that way does it folks. Well, I'm gone Q, until next time people. Peace. Love. Truth. Respect. Righteousness. Wisdom. And first and for most GOD the father and creator.

Always,

Errol V. Moore Jr.

98. WRITINGS / JOURNAL LOG (3.34) Brain Storming Ideas for writing

Let's Build!!!

5 year into the millennium

Just 140 years from slavery

That's like right around the corner

In terms of time

Tear that wool from your eyes

All you have to do

Is use your ears

Open your eyes

Don't be surprised

It's been right in front of you

Now it's time to react

Let's go get it

Stand up!!!

Let them know it won't be

SLAVERY !!!!!!!!!!!!!!!!!!!

Was considered to be entirely illegal.
My great-grandmothers and fathers experienced life as a slave.
I see now why my grandmother Eslin Francis was bitter about her past.
(Anger engraved from being enslaved.
Having it run through your veins with no escape from the nuece.
)

There were at least 4,730 lynchings in the United States, including some 3,440 black men and women. Most of these were in the post-Reconstruction South between 1882 and 1944, where southern whites used lynching and other terror tactics to intimidate blacks into political, social, and economic submission. Contrary to a widespread misconception, only about a quarter of lynch victims were accused of rape or attempted rape. Most blacks were lynched for outspokenness or other presumed offenses against whites, or in the aftermath of race riots. In many cases lynchings were not spontaneous mob violence but involved a degree of planning and law-enforcement cooperation. Racially motivated lynchings, which often involved the mutilation and immolation of the victim, might be witnessed by an entire local community as a diverting spectacle.

Can you believe that S#T!*

State and local governments in the South did little to curtail lynchings; various laws against mob violence were seldom enforced. Three times (1922, 1937, 1940) antilynching legislation passed the House of Representatives, only to be defeated in the Senate. Although the term has fallen into disuse since the civil-rights movement of the 1960s, similar practices still occur, often classified today as "bias crimes."

We're still slaves

  Wake up!

    My brother

    My sister

      From the strong holds.

        PEACE,

         -E MO'

99. WRITINGS / JOURNAL LOG (3.35)

A letter to Umoja (the mother of black unity),

I will start this off by saying to you that I love you and nothing has ever changed. In that though I would like to discuss a few issues I see within our relationship. I don't understand what clicks or causes things to go south with us but, it is pretty frustrating dealing with this imbalance. Umoja, are you happy with the life you lead at this point. It does seem that there is a hidden agenda with you, your attitude and communications with me. Every little incident we encounter seems to grow thru maybe your lack of understanding of the situation or like I said prior; there must be a hidden agenda. I do take responsibility for my tongue but at the same time do you take responsibility for yours? Why is it that, my tongue is to be so slow and yours so fast? I know sometimes I speak to you like a brother speaks to his sister and I have even said, "shut up". I can admit my faults and I know that I need to work on those specifics.

There are several areas that you need to work on as well. First: It is not right nor is it responsible to direct the children in an opposition towards me. I don't care what is said, if you have an issue with me, let's direct that within the two of us, that's what they call communication. To allow yourself to call out the father of those children, on a matter, which we can confront on our own, is a tad immature and should be understood by you. Second: How am I supposed to remain attentive and stable in this relationship when you get so head strong that any point you make has to remain stone and anyone who opposes, or holds a stance that offers a small resistance against what you feel, causes at the time major static. Third: I am a man, I am dedicated to my family, I have nothing but my all to give but you question my efforts and me. For you Umoja, to tell me "I'm tired of carrying you, and things are not just going to be set up for you", to me is slap in the face as a man, who is a provider, teacher, protector, and guide. I don't know what it is that you are going thru but, it sounds like we need to fix and or chime in to what that may be together. Fourth: The issue we crossed today was one that should've been quieted before it went there. I did not appreciate bringing up my decease grand parents to have you speak on them as if you know everything, or as if you have the key to knowledge and understanding. I don't care how high your educational status may be, it does not equate to rational timing and good sense towards life and its full meaning for us as human beings.

Umoja, sometimes you speak a good game when it comes to the black household or family of today but, you still must understand you have a lot to learn my sweet. Don't rush into your thoughts, seek wisdom, build on that and then speak. Why? I ask would you be put off by my mockery of proper etiquette. Does it offend you that much to where; you would get heated over the matter? I overstood your rational behind your ingrained beliefs and implementation towards the children but let us use some understanding of certain situations as they arise. We do tend to as people trying to obtain or uphold a certain criteria take things far to serious sometimes. Also, I would like to let you know that no! I will and never have been anything like the men in my mother's past, so for you to say, "Your acting like those men that you despised as a child" is a foolish statement for you to let come out from the unders of your mind. For you even to compare me is a major misrepresentation of my ability's and blessings that GOD has sat at my feet to spread throughout my family and to those in need of them. I'm a little wiser now in my reactions towards some of your poor thought out slants as crass as they might be sometimes. Umoja, a lot of men in my position might not be so nice and reserve my love. Regardless though, I want us to talk and come to agreements together not divide our eye contact and communication. Let's cut off all this negative crap going on around us and focus on this beautiful family and relationship the LORD has blessed us with. Let's be smart in our decisions as adults and as husband and wife.

I Love You Consistently,
Errol

100. WRITINGS / JOURNAL LOG (3.36)

Termination Telecommunications

(A final statement letter written to SBC and to (California Workers of America) upon my termination from employment with SBC.)

To whom it may concern:

I know that I may have deviated slightly from SBC set rules and policies but, do to my being a creature of habit (a human being), a hard worker and not a robot or a clone, I feel firmly that the powers that be whom have cast judgment upon me have not given me a fair shake in my current situation. I take full responsibility for giving my body, my sweat, precious time with my kids and family, and sometimes my blood to this company. Upon entry into SBC, I was not only privileged to find employment with one of the top telecommunication companies in the world but I also vowed to give my opportunity every chance for success. Although; I came in underpaid within a new subsidiary of SBC, I gave myself to ASI (Advanced Solutions Inc.), before being surplused out into another position within SBC. The training received during my transition period I must say was mediocre at best. What I'd thought was top of the line training, had turned out to be nothing but simulation boards and instruction that had been contracted out to retired employees. So, as I was thrust into the position of installation and repair technician I found the field of work to be somewhat overwhelming, not just in the physical aspect of the job but the knowledge that I lacked never was properly expanded with the appropriate help needed. In addition to my lack of knowledge I had been placed under the guidance and supervision of inexperienced technicians whom had less than five years with the company and less than that as installation and repair technicians, not to mention the supervisors, whom also were in experimental stages of knowledge within their respective position. Coming from such places as marketing into a role that required much more field experience and knowledge to be fully effective, didn't allow for adequate job assistance in terms of having the answers for certain situations in the field or knowing who to contact when an issue of any type had developed.

So after four years of work I found myself reaching out for additional training and assistance but never found any until my employment with the company had become somewhat unstable. Constant PDP issues, threats to placed on PIP programs and possible suspensions without pay if my numbers didn't meet the ever-changing company expectations, added tremendous stress on my mind and my body leaving me in an unhealthy state of being. I found little assistance until my situation got out of hand. And now here we are today. Due to my under productive numbers I became an object of speculation, ridicule, and a target to be used as an example. Although; I gave myself everyday to this company, the fact that an alleged falsification of my timesheets and GPS documentation of my whereabouts during company time, even after video taped surveillance, is the dirt that has been dug up and now used as the main ingredient to decide the fate of my employment, I feel is a cheap move given to an employee who bust his butt to get the job done. If my whereabouts clearly show me not falsifying but working tirelessly, willing out most jobs, often times doing the work of two or three men and providing excellent customer service for SBC, why snag me like some lifeless worm on hook for slight deviations which show me on those days doing my JOB.

I end my statement by saying, "If I was giving a fighters chance to erase my deviations of company procedure I would do so, If I was told to climb one hundred poles, string fifty drop lines, install eighty jacks, and earn a minimum of one hundred ERIC credits within an eight hour work day I would do so also. I guess what I'm saying is that, whatever was required of me I never resisted the call, I never deviated from my duty as first an employee of SBC and second a living breathing human being.

Errol V. Moore Jr.
9\7\04   12:03 pm
*Employed 11\28\99
*Terminated 9\17\04

101. WRITINGS / JOURNAL LOG (3.37)

The Superstar That Never Was

Everybody knows about Michael Jordan, Barry Bonds, Jerry Rice, and a list of bonified big names, the ultimate of elite athletes in their sport, but every year thousands of athletes graduate from high school or college and you rarely hear their story as they fall from glory to common experiences becoming role models in occupations far from the media and attention of the mass crowds of fans. They take on a wide variety of roles that keep our nation and its economy moving, impacting virtually every family, yet the focus remains on the few, less than 1% of the population, while 99% of ordinary people will never experience, other than in their fantasies, the euphoria of the superstar. In my youth I had the privilege of competing with and against some of the most talented athletes in the nation and the list of names would be impossible to recall, but for those who read this book, you know who you are, so this is dedicated to you, my sons, and yours, who probably never had a real opportunity to fulfill their professional dreams.

We have lost touch with reality as the Tiger Woods story propels parents to create super athletes at the expense of out of control lifestyles and schedules, forcing activity to replace productivity, too often, failing to stop and review the direction and values of family quality. Every family can't have a Venus and Serena story manifested to reality, so what will it cost you to pursue the unattainable. We have reduced the value of a girl who perhaps has a goal to be a wonderful housewife, and loving mother who's impact collectively of every generation, affects the direction of a nation, even the whole world. The fallout of the liberated woman of the 70's has already created independent individuality that has disrupted family loyalty and many young women today, some already with children are declaring no interest in ever being married, with a delusional theory of being capable of raising children alone...go ahead, wear yourself out before you're 30 and become hard, cold, and callused, at least you can find a man when you need one for sex. Is that all you feel you deserve? When the kids have gone, what is the empty nest syndrome you hear about? Well, you have your career, your own home, and a late model car, and some have turned to other women and the pride of denial has ripped off your future, the fulfillment of complete intimacy only a loving husband can share in the twilight of your years.

I'm sure as a young boy playing anywhere we could create a competition, in the street, the hallway, front or back yard, most often battling my older brother, which drove me to a higher level, and sometimes even against my sisters, which I'm sure improved their athletic skills and actually permitted me to perform in a more relaxed level of competition from the intensity of my brothers pressure. We could imitate Mays, McCovey, Clemente, Aaron, White, Marichal, Perry, Colfax, Drysdale, Gibson, Brock or Wills. We practiced game winning hits, Giants vs. Dodgers, with Vin Scully, Russ Hodges or Lon Simmons and the cry of " bye, bye, baby "or "the 2-2 pitch... is hit deep to left aaannnnd that one is gone", was a normal sound echoing in the neighborhood, and I could almost vividly hear the roar of a packed out Candlestick or Chavez Ravine. We practiced 2 out, 3-2 count, bottom of the 9th situations and it become normal to get the game-winning hit. As my exposure grew in the area sports programs, I had the privilege of competing against players like Dusty Baker, Jerry Royster, Jerry Manual, Randy Lerch, Nyls Nyman, Taylor Duncan, Leon Lee, Derick Lee's father, and had early childhood playmates like Roland Office, Leland Glass, and Bob Forsch. It wasn't just baseball, Darnell Hillman and Joe Kemp in basketball, and Otis Cooper and Lou Harris as well as other former pro and major league players.

After returning to Sac City, having completed a tour in Viet Nam in 71, drafted by the Phillies in the winter of 72, and being released after just 2 weeks of spring training in Clearwater, Florida, I contacted Bob Forsch while there and he put me up in his home for a few days and arranged a tryout for me with the Cardinals, but I was so demoralized, I returned home without going to the invitation Bob had arranged. Sometimes you need a mentor or father to advise you when dreams have been shattered, yet opportunity is still present through another door you hadn't imagined. Thanks Bob, for being a true friend and going the extra mile. Bob gave me a ticket to a Cardinals vs. Braves game while there, and after concluding a brief conversation with Dusty, Hank Aaron while passing in left field nodded hello. Later during the game, a grounder foul off Hank's bat came towards me and as I reached over the rail to catch it in my bare left hand, the whole stadium seemed to notice and roared with laughter of approval of the nonchalant effort as I tossed the ball to a little boy coming towards me...15 seconds of fame, and a dream abandoned.

To my youngest son Terrell,

I apologize to all the sons of fathers who shared their dreams of becoming professional athletes and somehow we were not able to launch you in the proper places to further the opportunity you deserved. You fulfilled the discipline and physical commitment to accomplish your goal, but we failed to emotionally support you with good judgment and wise decision-making. Not because we couldn't see your potential, but because we allowed the issues of our own dilemma to distract us at crucial points where you needed to be directed and encouraged. History does repeat itself when we don't learn life's lessons, so I pray someday you can be the perfect father and example for your own children.

-Errol Moore Sr.   (2004)

Errol Van Moore Jr.

The Artist, The Poet, The Song Writer, The Entertainer. Born in 1974, Errol comes off without question as a well-seasoned performer and writer. Originally from the capitol of California in Sacramento. Errol, a.k.a. Belevm, has continued to establish himself as a well-rounded entertainer in the art of spoken word, rap, dance, and acting for over fourteen plus years. He has gained an enormous wealth of experience thru the many rigors and challenges he has faced within the music and entertainment industry. He prides himself in having a limitless creative concept base, coupled with various styles of word play, off figured lyrical techniques and a call to the stage of entertainment. Errol, holds fast to a tremendous faith and an undying will and spirit that will make him a sought out force to be seen and heard on a global scale. Errol has been performing since 1989. He has won numerous talent shows, and has entertained thousands of people.

Notable performances include:

San Francisco, CA. - Convention Center\ Music and Actors Guild & Awards Show

(Which included the cast from the movie, Five Heartbeats, School Daze and other established actors, radio personalities and musicians)

Richmond, Ca. - Martin Luther King Jr. Birthday Celebration\ performed before the likes of Coretta Scott King and a host of political figures and dignitaries.

Miami, Fl. - Bobby Jones Gospel Show\ featuring: Kirk Franklin and others

Other notable performances:

Oakland, Ca. (performed w/ Sega Genesis spokes person and rapper, Chilly E.B., & Rapper Forte') /

UC Berkeley & SFU (performed with acts such as The Living Legends (Mystic Journey Men), Mac Mall, & Aceyalone

(Hometown performances) Sacramento, Ca.
* Heritage Festivals sponsored by: KBMB 103.5 "The Bomb"
* Sacramento State University's Hip-hop Showcase 1, 2 and 3 (performed with acts such as: The Coup, The Bumz, Three Six Mafia & ILL and AL Scratch)

- Perkins Hall w/ The Hieroglyphics Crew (Souls of Mischief, Pep Love, and Del tha Funke Homosapien)
- The Grind (skateboard park) – w/ Redman, Keith Murray and Krs One.

Errol Van Moore SR.

The War Veteran, The Artist & The Athlete. Born in 1950, in Decatur, ILL. Errol continues to exercise his creativity through his oil paintings and writings. He is in search for inspirational experiences in life as he ages upon mother earth. Residing in Sacramento, California Errol was once considered to be one of the City of Sacramento, top baseball players throughout his high school days at Hiram Johnson, to his collegiate and MLB farm league experiences. Now enjoying his present years, watching his grandchildren as they grow and continue to entertain him with their athletic inheritances and multitude of talents. Errol fully understands first hand that life is full of obstacles and challenges, as he has most recently been diagnosed as being a pre-diabetic.

www.ingramcontent.com/pod-product-compliance
Lightning Source LLC
Chambersburg PA
CBHW061351280526
45784CB00001B/216